City Vineyard

A church bears fruit in inner London

by Chris & Sue Brown

Foreword by Terry Virgo

Harvestime

Published in the United Kingdom by:
Harvestime Services Ltd, 12a North Parade, Bradford
West Yorkshire BD1 3HT

First published by Harvestime
First printed November 1989

Also referred to: Revised Standard Version (RSV)

British Library Cataloguing in Publication Data

Brown, Chris
City vineyard.
1. Great Britain. Urban regions. Inner areas. Christian church. Evangelism
I. Title II. Brown, Sue
269'.2'0941

ISBN 0-947714-79-0

Typeset in the United Kingdom by:
E. Thompson (Typesetters) Ltd., Bradford BD8 7BX
Printed and bound in the United Kingdom by:
Richard Clay Ltd., Bungay, Suffolk

Contents

To
Pauline, Graham, David, Timothy and Andrew

Foreword

Few tasks can be more demanding than leading a small church in the inner city in England today. It requires real faith to get started and powerful steadfastness to keep going.

Chris and Sue Brown have proved their worth by sticking with it until their church, lying under the shadow of London's Tower Bridge, has prospered and grown, proving that God's power will prevail, whatever the circumstances, if we do things his way.

I recommend this book for any who feel they are facing an uphill battle – whether it be in the inner city, in the sprawling housing estates surrounding some of our major towns, or even in sleepy country villages. Every situation provides its own unique challenge. But if we are sure God has sent us, we can expect ultimate success, providing we refuse to give in to unbelief and discouragement.

Conversions are always a miracle of God's grace, wherever they happen. Chris and Sue's story reminds us that we must keep our eyes on a sovereign God and refuse to be overawed by the apparent giants of impossibility in our modern concrete jungles.

Their story also shows key turning-points where God's promptings resulted in vital breakthroughs. How important it is, in the midst of dogged endurance and obedience to biblical building-patterns, also to remain sensitive in order to hear God's fresh word and act upon it.

I pray that many will find inspiration in the pages of this book and that many new churches will be planted and built to the glory of God in our land.

Terry Virgo

November 1989

Preface

We have had a growing conviction that God wanted us to write down this story about the establishing of one church in London's inner city: Vineyard Community Church.

We were finding that newer Christians within the church knew little or nothing about how God had worked to bring it about. As we related the story to various people we got excited, and so did they. It has seemed right and scriptural to pass it on as a record.

We also know of small churches and missions still struggling, not having learnt some of the lessons which have proved so dynamic to us. For these, we pray that reading of our experience will encourage and illuminate their own church life.

We want to spark vision and faith for the inner city. We didn't experience instant success; it was an uphill struggle. But we have a great God who takes very ordinary people and works through them.

We don't claim to have everything in perfect perspective. Nor do we believe that our view is the only one. We do know that God has worked a miracle in the inner city and it has been great to be a part of it.

For ease of reading we have written this together as a personal story but, in order to maintain clarity, we have written in the first person as from Chris. We pray that it will stir you in whatever way God wants.

Chris and Sue Brown
November 1989

See how great a flame aspires,
Kindled by a spark of grace!
Jesus' love the nations fires,
Sets the kingdoms on a blaze.
To bring fire on earth he came;
Kindled in some hearts it is:
O that all might catch the flame,
All partake the glorious bliss!

When he first the work began,
Small and feeble was his day:
Now the word doth swiftly run,
Now it wins its widening way;
More and more it spreads and grows,
Ever mighty to prevail;
Sin's strongholds it now o'erthrows,
Shakes the trembling gates of hell.

Sons of God, your Saviour praise!
He the door hath opened wide;
He hath given the word of grace,
Jesu's word is glorified;
Jesus, mighty to redeem,
He alone the work hath wrought;
Worthy is the work of him,
Him who spake a world from nought.

Saw ye not the cloud arise,
Little as a human hand?
Now it spreads along the skies,
Hangs o'er all the thirsty land:
Lo! the promise of a shower
Drops already from above;
But the Lord will shortly pour
All the Spirit of his love.

– *Charles Wesley, 1707-88*

1

Then and now

'They're enjoying themselves,' the lady commented, laughing, as she passed by with her full shopping trolley.

'That's our church,' said Sue with pleasure and pride. 'The one that meets here,' she added, nodding towards our Drummond Road building.

'Oh, we've often heard you singing.'

It was a bright, sunny morning in June. Vineyard Community Church were out in force in Bermondsey, London, for a Saturday morning praise march. Their bright clothes, smiling faces and lively singing – accompanied by musicians on the back of a lorry – made the procession attractive.

Children were loving it all. Banners were held aloft bearing the name of the church or slogans such as 'Choose life, choose Jesus!' Church folk in clowns outfits gave out leaflets and balloons.

Most of the hundred and twenty present had started the march with a mixture of excitement and nervousness, but none would have missed it. This was their chance joyfully and publicly to praise God and witness to his goodness in their lives and church. They were excited with what God was doing.

Here was a glorious mixture of inner-city people, all shapes and sizes, cultures and backgrounds, all at various stages of maturity but all 'going out with joy and being led forth in peace'.

Where had they all come from? Some were students living and studying in London. Some were new Christians. Others had deliberately looked for a 'live' church where they could actively worship during their stay in London. Still others were post-graduates who, having caught the vision for the inner city, had found jobs in local schools or hospitals.

A number had come to work with the London City Mission on their Voluntary Evangelism Scheme. They, too, had caught the vision and settled down in Vineyard, some now with families in tow.

Others were born and bred in Bermondsey, Walworth or Rotherhithe and had been converted a number of years before. They had faithfully followed God through many changes and could look back with thankfulness.

Still more were fairly new Christians, joining in with great enthusiasm after God had completely changed their lives. One was a London taxi driver who, the day following his daughter's baptism, met with God in his taxi-cab. Still shedding tears of joy and emotion, he had telephoned his wife at home.

'God has just met with me,' he had managed to tell her.

'Yes, and the same thing has just happened to me,' she had replied, also through tears.

There was the couple whose lives had been in a complete mess through drugs and alcohol. Their marriage had been faltering. Then God had stepped in and made them whole. Now they were at peace with themselves and very happy with God. The emaciated husband was putting on weight, completely free of drugs and having only the occasional battle with alcohol. They were a happy family unit.

There was the couple who had been on the verge of splitting up when God saved them. They and their three children were all with us on the praise march. They had been through a lot of racial harassment from neighbours on the estate where they lived, but they were still following God and proving his grace.

There was the man who had come to a Sunday morning service with his wife and received a vision from God. It had shaken him. He had come face to face with the God who loved him and wanted his love in return.

There was the lady who had been shown very little love in her childhood. On receiving a gift of groceries from her homegroup she had broken down and wept.

'Now I have a family who really care for me,' she had said. 'God is making it all up to me.'

There was the lady whose chronic arthritis had been healed by God at her conversion. Wheelchair and walking-sticks had been given away.

So the list could go on – people who had been delivered from all sorts of corruption in the world and who were still being delivered as they offered their lives daily to God.

'See how these Christians love one another,' commented more than one visitor to the church. Yes, God had done something tremendous. We were a family together, loving and caring for one another. And the march was a great opportunity to sing his praise and point others to him.

It wasn't always like this

Later that day, after the praise march, Sue and I looked back. Not only were we excited by the day's events but we felt a sense of fulfilment. Before our eyes we had seen the church established. To us it was a miracle. Twenty-five years ago it hadn't been like this.

We remembered some typical 'open air witness' from those days. A mere handful of people ventured out rather self-consciously to the corner of the street. We carried a dark box which, though it looked a bit like a coffin, was in fact a harmonium. With the organist seated, we were ready to begin. We sang our praise to God sincerely enough, after which someone would testify personally to God's goodness, followed by a short gospel message.

Usually a few children tagged along to watch. A few faces peered around curtains. Pedestrians hurried by embarrassed – doubly so if they were recognised.

But we felt good. We had overcome our fear. The gospel had been proclaimed. Maybe someone would respond, though in truth we didn't expect much.

Ours was typical of so many inner-city Christian works at that time. A steady decline had set in over a number of years.

We were struggling to keep up activities so that people had a chance to respond to God. We believed that the gospel was his good news for these folk, but our experience did not encourage a lot of faith.

'Hold the fort' and 'Keep the light shining' were the mottoes at that time. After all, what could we few do against so much evil in this densely populated area?

'I'm coming to your Sunday school now,' a small boy once told us. 'This is the third one I've been to. The other two both closed. I'll come to yours until it closes.'

We had smiled ruefully. Certainly ours was a struggling work but we weren't going to give up easily.

The work in question was at Lansdowne Place Medical Mission – 'Lansdowne' for short and known as 'the Mission' by all the local people.

I was involved there for many years, having come originally with my father to help with boys' Bible classes and clubs. We lived at West Norwood, further out in the suburbs. Still in my teens, I felt a bit scared by the roughness of the area, but I was deeply challenged by the needs of the place and excited by the sense of 'mission'. Although the boys were unruly I enjoyed their quick-wittedness and fun and I grew to love them.

A number of years passed. One particular journey up to the Mission from West Norwood stands out clearly in my mind. It must have been some twenty-five years before the praise march.

I was caught in a traffic jam in the Old Kent Road. Ahead in the distance I could see the new Post Office Tower. To my right and left, by contrast, were busy, dirty, noisy, run-down streets. The two views seemed to symbolise the two sides of London: the sharp contrast between the high-pressure, go-ahead city life and the mundane, seemingly apathetic way of life of the ordinary people.

Then some words came to my mind from Isaiah 55: 'Instead of the thornbush will grow the pine tree, and instead of briers the myrtle will grow.'

The words came to me as both a promise and a commission. God wanted to do something in that densely-packed part of London and I knew that I was to give myself to the task. When, earlier, I had offered myself for missionary service abroad, the advice of the godly elders of my home church had been that my missionary calling was to London.

This 'concrete jungle' was certainly a thorny, barren wilderness as far as spiritual growth was concerned. But God was saying that it wasn't always going to be that way. The 'pine' and 'myrtle' are evergreens, symbolic of perpetual spiritual life.

So I gave myself to co-operate with God in bringing it about. I wanted to live wholeheartedly for him wherever he wanted. Sue joined me in that vision.

How the change took place

God has worked in his people in this inner city. The church today bears little resemblance to that of a quarter of a century ago. For one thing, morale is higher.

'No-one could miss the zeal, love and fervour for the Lord that you all have,' commented one lady who later joined us. 'There's a real sense of going on with God and his life being expressed through you.'

Whenever someone asks us what has happened here, we get excited all over again as we relate the story. We tell our story here to encourage your faith for the church in the inner city, and to pass on some of the lessons we have learnt. We claim no credit. We just feel a deep gratitude to God for the privilege of being one small part of his vast purpose in the world.

The New Testament portrays churches that were dynamic with a sense of God's presence, meeting people where they were and seeing lives transformed. We believe that such churches are possible today, bringing purpose, community, love, hope, joy, righteousness and justice to bear upon the problems of hopelessness, hate, injustice, misery and loneliness in our inner cities.

Some people believe that, if you want to influence a nation, you should start with the universities. Jesus, however, started with 'the common people'. His message was 'good news to the *poor*'. And Paul tells us the sort of people Jesus used to 'turn the world upside down' in his day: 'Not many of you were wise by human standards,' he observes; 'not many were influential; not many were of noble birth' (see 1 Corinthians 1:26-31).

The same was true in later generations. It was following George Whitefield's preaching to miners at Kingswood that the Methodist revival really began to take off. More recently, the Salvation Army and the Pentecostals have touched our church and nation largely through ordinary working people.

The place is important, too. Jesus may have started out in tiny Nazareth, but he finished in the *city* – in Jerusalem. And it was in that city that the Holy Spirit was poured out, at a time when 'God-fearing Jews from every nation' were visiting. Later, the apostles, in their Holy-Spirit-directed strategy for evangelism, headed for the major cities and centres of communication.

When Jesus said, 'Go and make disciples of all nations', he meant 'peoples', not geographical nation-states. Where do we find representatives of many nations, peoples and tongues today? In our cities.

Our taxi driver talks about Jesus to passengers from all over the world. Our medical people in London hospitals treat patients from many different countries. Others live next door to people who have friends and relatives around the globe. The possibilities are endless.

In our church in Bermondsey about ten nations are represented. A local doctor told us that he had seen patients of at least twenty different nationalities within two weeks of his starting general practice in our area.

I am convinced there are good reasons for giving our inner cities high priority. There may not be such a quick, obvious impact as in the establishment of a lively church in a small town but, long term, the impact can be many times greater.

2

Living in the city

Sue was taking the children to school. She met up with another parent and they walked along together. They were halfway across Tower Bridge Road when the lady asked, 'You don't come from London, do you?'

'No, I come from Dorset,' Sue replied.

'Why ever did you come to London from a lovely place like Dorset?' she exclaimed.

'Because we feel this is where God wants us to be.'

The lady's mouth dropped open and her cigarette remained poised in mid-air halfway to it. If Sue had suddenly hit her she couldn't have looked more surprised. Such a concept was completely new to her.

We had received a variety of comments from well-meaning friends or relatives when they heard that we planned to settle in inner London – comments like, 'You won't bring the children up there, surely, will you?' Some felt we were taking a risk and being a little irresponsible.

Fortunately we had encouragement and prayer support from others who knew, as we did, that we could trust God for our children and ourselves wherever we were. Missionaries called to serve God overseas faced the same kind of difficulties in an even bigger way. If God had called us, he would take care of us. We saw it as a missionary call and, yes, it would mean sacrifice on our part, but we wanted to follow God.

During my early days of involvement with Lansdowne I had come to some firm convictions about the way forward. I became convinced that, if a lasting work was to be done, we would have to sink our lives into the city and become part of it. 'Hit and run' evangelism, however earnest and enthusiastic, just would not do. God himself didn't shout at the world through a loudhailer. He sent his Son to live right among us.

Earlier, I had been inspired by a missionary biography about a group of Christians in Tokyo. They had sold their homes and all moved to a poorer part of the city to start a church there. Surely that was the only way. Naturally we would have preferred green fields and less noise and dirt, but God wanted us in Bermondsey.

Long-term stay

I had also decided that our commitment should be long-term. So many inner-city churches had suffered from the blight of 'stepping-stone' pastors, especially in nonconformist churches.

Young men, straight from college, often started their ministries in small, run-down city churches. They gained useful experience, no doubt, but in most cases used it only to further their careers elsewhere. Sometimes they were men of outstanding ability, and churches would flourish for a time under their leadership, only to be left to flounder after they had moved on.

One of my uncles had described me as 'a plodder'. At the time, a period of patient plodding was the very thing the church needed. Later on, I was asked to be the pastor and I felt I needed to give it ten years. If after ten years nothing had been built, however, I would take it that God was not in it and would think again. Sue, temperamentally, was not a plodder and had to learn much patience over the time in Bermondsey!

The local church – God's way

Another strong conviction of mine – one that has grown through the years – is that society can only be affected through the establishing of strong local churches.

Looking back, I can see that there were large gaps in my understanding of what 'church' meant, but I did see that church-planting was the New Testament method. People are best reached for Christ through the life and witness of their own kind, and the local church is therefore the best means of evangelism.

So it was that, when Sue and I were first married, we looked for a place to live as near as possible to the Mission.

We were excited and nervous at the same time. We almost felt we were in a different country. At first the nearest place we could get was in Peckham, but six months afterwards we were able to move into a flat near the Borough tube station. It was a real introduction to inner-city life. Our flat was on the top floor of a block which had no lifts and no baths.

Our daughter was born during our short stay there. Sue found it hard getting baby and shopping up the fifty-two stairs! At least we had a shed at the bottom to house the pram. We also had the luxury of a washing-line. It was quite a novelty to hang the clothes on the flat roof between the chimney stacks.

Noise could be a problem. It was not all sweetness and light between the couple who lived beneath us, and the sound of their rows frequently rose through the floorboards.

Some people kept the stairs beautifully clean while others neglected them completely. But most of the folk were reasonably friendly, and it was good that another Christian family lived in the same block.

After a year, the opportunity came to move into the first floor at Lansdowne, over the medical department. We took it. At that time, I had a full-time job with a missionary publishing society in Victoria. The pay wasn't fantastic but the rent for the flat was small, and we managed.

Living in the Mission

It was good living there – only a dozen stairs! We had a small roof garden around which we erected a fence to give our children a play space. We also grew a few flowers.

Our door opened immediately opposite the patients' waiting-room. Sue came downstairs one morning to go shopping, and was greeted by a blunt comment from a disgruntled patient: 'I hope they never give me a flat underneath you!' Apparently the patter of tiny feet upstairs hadn't been very soothing to the unwell lady!

Dr Oxford and Nurse Turner seemed to enjoy our family being around but we had to encourage the children not to make too much noise when surgery was in progress.

Living there helped us to understand some of the problems faced by most of our neighbours. Almost everyone in the area lived in council flats. We were surrounded by blocks mostly four or five storeys high, making up Tabard Gardens Estate. These 'lovely, modern' flats had been built before the war to replace the previous back-to-back, multi-occupied slum houses.

'Like a rabbit warren on a cliff face' was how a friend described one block, as he watched the numerous inhabitants popping in and out of their front doors on the landings.

Washing put out on lines was liable to be nicked. Sheds built to house bicycles or prams were prone to be broken into. Arguments, loud music, children with no garden to play in romping on the floor over the home of a night worker or elderly person – these are just a few of the in-built tensions of living on top of one another.

Bored gangs of youths, thrown together by crowded conditions, spent their time roaming around looking for something to do. Among favourite pastimes were vandalising old cars, writing on walls and throwing stones at the Mission. The high truancy rate didn't help. Neither did the general acceptance that not much could be done about the area's problems.

'I keep myself to myself' was a frequently-heard comment. Sometimes this reflected the selfish attitude of people who didn't want to be involved with others. More frequently it showed an understandable inability to cope with the sheer pressure of always having others so near. Privacy was often hard to come by.

About the time we moved into Lansdowne, different nationalities started to move into the district. Until then it had been a white, working class area. More tensions ensued.

'I want some grass to walk on'

We had a few trees around and a few local parks, but the overall absence of green affected us all a lot.

'Mummy, I want to go for a walk and I want some grass to walk on,' said our first son one day. He said it quite emphatically, almost defiantly, because he felt the lack so much.

We had both been brought up to appreciate the countryside and passed this on to our children. We learned to take regular time off away from the city. Although we had very little money, God always gave us places to go and we enjoyed some lovely holidays with our children. When we came to the end of those times away it took a determined effort of will to get into the car and drive home.

Sue recalls on one occasion coming back into London on the train from Reading. She became aware that her spirits were dropping more and more the nearer she got to home. The oppressiveness of the city is a force to be reckoned with.

Some people say you have to love the city to be able to serve the Lord there. We confess to a love-hate relationship. God gave us a love for it but we didn't always like it!

At times we were sickened by the number of children who were neglected and left so much to themselves. Or by the state of lonely old people, a few of whom lay dead in their flats for weeks before anyone noticed they were missing.

Open home

When Sue became a Christian at the age of fifteen, God

quickly opened her eyes to the tremendous blessing of having an open, Christian home. The Lord was not known in her home at that time and she became very aware of the peace of the Christian homes she visited. She vowed that when she had a home of her own it would be used for God. Career would be secondary, home primary.

Her convictions fitted in well with my expectations. My own parents had always had an open home and I took it for granted that ours would be the same.

So it was that our Lansdowne flat, first the upstairs one and later the one on the ground floor, was well used. I felt that our kitchen, where people used to pop in for tea or coffee, was as important as the meeting-hall. After going full-time, I often came downstairs from my office to find people enjoying fellowship together. There were very few of us Christians around and we needed one another a lot.

Values – middle-class or God's?

The Lord blessed us over the years with five children. Each arrival elicited the usual jokes: 'If you can't get other people into the Mission you can fill it with your family!'

It wasn't easy bringing them up in what was sometimes a hostile environment. Perhaps we were a little naive when we first said we knew we could trust God for our children. Praise him, he has proved faithful to us. We have been put to the test and been able to overcome through his grace.

We constantly needed wisdom. Our speech, the way we spent our money, the way we treated others, our table manners and our wanting to follow God marked us out from the people who surrounded us. We were constantly re-evaluating our behaviour. Which of our values were merely middle-class and which were God's?

It was heartbreaking at times to see the jealousy and spite aimed at our children by neighbours or classmates. People viewed us with suspicion. To them we were middle-class oddities who talked differently, had received a better upbringing and would therefore look down on them.

According to their thinking, our religion was part of our background, so believing in God was easier for us! Most of them didn't think that God was interested in them, or that our religion had anything relevant to say. When I once asked a group of teenagers how they would recognise a Christian, the answer came back: 'Drinkless, smokeless and talks posh'!

Not everyone was unfriendly but it took time for us to be accepted as part of the community. Slowly, as our children grew up and attended local schools, we were treated more normally.

Life in the Mission

In 1968, the small group of Christians at Lansdowne asked me to be their full-time pastor. I accepted, knowing already that God had called me to the work.

Sue and I were then living in the flat above the medical wing. She was with me totally in my vision. Although there was a cost to us, we felt Lansdowne was a good place to be and we were following in a good tradition. It had started and continued as a labour of love to serve people.

Being in the middle of the council estate, Lansdowne was very community-conscious. Its life had always been characterised by social concern. In fact, the original hall had been opened in 1852 as a Ragged School by the Seventh Earl of Shaftesbury.

Reading some of the historical accounts is fascinating. The opening of the Ragged School had been well advertised beforehand. When the Sunday evening arrived, so did masses of children – 'half-naked . . . Arabs,' one writer called them.

'When the door opened they rushed in with wild excitement,' he continued. 'In an instant the room was packed. Everyone shouted or whistled his loudest, each trying to outdo the other . . . . The weather was warm and bright and, for the purpose of preventing escape, the front door was closed . . . . The atmosphere was not one of a garden of roses – the sickening odours arising from their filthy rags and the rich perfumes oozing from every pore of their unwashed, foul bodies caused one or two of the girls to faint.'

The work continued through the years. God's love was expressed practically, teaching the children, helping the needy and preaching the gospel. There were the soup kitchens, the penny bank, help for the handicapped and clubs for all ages, as well as cheap outings.

During the 1930s the medical wing was opened. As there was no National Health Service in those days, the Mission paid the doctor and nurse so that treatment could be given free to the local people. Dentistry, eye treatment, chiropody and massage were also available.

The Sunday school was large. The children were pleased to be doing something different and enjoyed the periodic treats. We have met Christians in many parts of the country who found the Lord in Bermondsey during that time.

One elderly, housebound lady, Mrs Bavin, had been converted through the Mission and delighted in telling me some of the tactics they used to employ. At one time, she recalled, there had been some adventurous evangelism. When pub closing time arrived the Christians were ready. Ushering the men and women into the Mission, they sobered them up with strong coffee, then preached the gospel to them with the aid of lantern slides.

The 1960s

Life within the Mission had changed by the 1960s. Numbers had dwindled and our evangelism was by no means as aggressive. No longer could we boast a large Sunday school but many other activities went on as before.

The medical practice was now run by the National Health Service, but still with Christian staff from the Mission. Generally, people were better off. Materialism began to replace the poverty and gave folk a false security. Free soup and cheap outings weren't needed any more and neither, apparently, was God.

'You only go to the Mission for what you can get out of them,' became the scornful accusation levelled by their fellows at the brave few who still came. There was apathy and indifference to God. We weren't meeting the needs and we felt impotent. Though we had a terrific message, very few were listening to it.

We were still in a 'mission hall' situation. The major decisions were taken by a council, nearly all of whose members came from outside the locality. They would advise on building and finance as well as on the general life of the Mission.

We were staffed mainly by Christians who commuted in from other areas – as my own family had at one time. In the Mission they were called 'the workers' and they certainly earned the label, working hard to maintain a full quota of activities. The halls and rooms in Lansdowne were in use every night of the week for various clubs and meetings.

'We need more workers,' was the constant cry. It seemed important to try to keep things going the way they had done in the 1930s. But suburban churches, the source of workers, had also declined and the supply of help was running dry.

For us, the children's clubs and holidays, though hard work, were in fact great fun. We once took a party of boys for a holiday on the coast. One of the local residents had put a box of windfall apples outside his front gate with a notice saying, 'Please help yourself.' The boys did: they took the whole box! We found them down the road selling the apples and giving the proceeds to one boy who was short of pocket-money.

On another occasion we had an excursion into the countryside. The party of girls got lost but returned to us later carrying armfuls of daffodils, which they had thought were growing wild. In fact, they weren't, but the girls found it difficult to believe that such a large piece of land could be someone's private garden.

In the 1960s we were still taking a few children on holiday who hadn't seen the sea before, and families who otherwise wouldn't have got a break away from home.

The 'gospel lift'

Very few Christians lived in the area. People who had been converted over the years became better workers as a result, prospered and moved out.

This process was known by some as the 'gospel lift'. It meant that very few of the local people had a clear idea of what being a Christian entailed. To them, the church was largely an alien institution existing for the convenience of christenings, weddings and funerals. What they saw and heard on these occasions bore no relation to life as they knew it. Its leaders were from another culture, middle class and educated.

New Christians converted through mission halls were supposed to be fed into 'proper' churches. This rarely happened. They found the churches strange and formal, and the missions were, after all, their spiritual homes. So those who didn't move out of the district stayed in the mission, to be fed only on a basic gospel diet which left them, as often as not, weak and immature.

As I came to full-time work at Lansdowne, my conviction to see a church established was strengthened. I would no longer even attempt to feed new Christians into established churches. Instead, we would establish a local church at Lansdowne.

It was an unwritten law that church leaders must have had theological training. That meant a high level of education. As valuable as it may be to have a trained mind, I could see that the effect on working-class Christians was to make them feel inferior. My plan was to see local leaders emerging. The Lord didn't only single out educated men like Paul; he also found working men like Peter and John and equipped them to lead his people.

The history of trade unions shows that the ordinary working class can produce leaders of great ability. I aimed to see a local church formed which would be self-governing, self-supporting and self-propagating.

Fortunately for us, Lansdowne was a Shaftesbury Society mission. We were given freedom to operate in the way we felt right, unlike some other organisations which have been hampered by strict trust deeds and the like.

Bible teaching

At my induction service in 1968 one of the messages from Acts 2:42 seemed to express our vision: 'They devoted themselves to the apostles' teaching and to the fellowship, to the breaking of bread and to prayer.'

That's where we were going. We believed God's Word and he quickened it in our hearts. I had a rich legacy of evangelical Bible teaching and now set out to pass it on. I knew that the New Testament pattern was the right one for our Mission and couldn't wait to see it happen.

I thought of the church primarily as a *teaching centre*. 'If the people receive proper instruction from the Bible, not just gospel preaching, then we will see a difference,' I had said at the time. (When, later, my efforts had not produced the desired effect, I had to ask God why.) So, in addition to all the other activities, I tried to give time to helping Christians understand the Bible.

Sue and I and a few others were excited by our vision. Many more just didn't understand what I was getting at. None of us realised how much we had to learn.

Though we may not have been clear in our understanding of what 'church' was meant to be, we did know that the apostles' teaching, fellowship, breaking of bread and prayer must become priorities. God had stirred us to see his church established and we believed it would happen.

3

The blessings of failure

'There's a new wind blowing through Lansdowne,' commented one of our ladies soon after I was appointed pastor. She voiced what many of us were feeling. We all had high hopes for the future.

Many friends believed – and frequently told us – that ours was a hard district and that it would be hard work. Far from being put off by these observations, we were spurred on by them. At thirty years of age, I felt I had the benefit of youth together with a measure of experience. I had a clear call from God coupled with an assurance that he would work through me. The Mission members confirmed my call; I was sure we could succeed.

My direction was to build a local church and I was confident it would happen. Looking back, I can see that my idea of 'church' was rather vague and much of my confidence was in using what I thought were the correct methods.

I had two main lines of approach: first, teaching and preaching from God's Word and, second, building up the young people.

Bible teaching came to form a major part of our meetings together. I was committed to systematic expository preaching and believed in its effectiveness. It was a powerful weapon which, when used faithfully, was bound to bring results. I was right – up to a point.

I asked God to help me make the message clear. Old-fashioned language and evangelical jargon had to go. Preaching must be relevant, with everyday illustrations. Bible studies would take place every week and the spiritual 'food' offered would include 'meat' – not just the 'milk' of a simple gospel message.

Lots of effort and manpower were ploughed into Sunday school and teens work. Our philosophy was, 'We'll get the children converted – they're more willing to come than the grown-ups – then we'll be able to nurture them and make them into mature, Christian adults.'

It proved to be a fallacy. With no support in school or home, the youngsters found it almost impossible to swim against the tide.

As for the teens, though, things seemed to go well for a while. They started attending the Sunday evening service along with a few other newer people. Some were also willing to help with the Sunday school or Bible classes. We were a little concerned about their lack of commitment, but surely we were halfway there? In those days, if you had *any* young people your church was considered successful.

What was 'church'?

When I began to talk about our need to become a church instead of a mission, most people weren't particularly thrilled with the idea. They immediately thought of some of the churches they knew.

These 'proper' churches were formal, dull places which made them feel uncomfortable and where people weren't over-friendly. They were expected to wear their best clothes and to talk in whispers while on the premises. The sermon usually contained words they couldn't understand and was altogether too highbrow to be interesting.

Some found it helpful to go to such churches, but most found it irrelevant. Christenings, weddings and funerals had to be borne with. Though some folk had dispensed with the first two, most didn't have a say in whether or not they attended their own funeral service! Locally, in fact, a lot was made of giving a person 'a good send-off' and the funerals were often quite grand affairs.

But on the whole 'going to church' was not done in Bermondsey.

Mission halls

Not being 'proper' churches, the mission halls were a law to themselves – ours included. They were more bright and breezy. We actually had chorus books as well as hymn books and sang heartily to the accompaniment of a piano instead of an organ. We had chairs instead of pews, though we still faced the front in rows.

It wasn't the normal practice, either, for people to come in and sit still before the meeting. A visitor on one occasion was amazed, on entering the hall, to see a man trimming another's eyebrows while waiting!

We remember the first time some teenage girls turned up wearing trousers. Horrors! How were they going to be received? Apart from a few stares, the incident passed by peacefully. We heard of other places where the same thing merited major concern. But we were far more happy-go-lucky. You didn't even have to wear your best clothes.

Although I took a certain pleasure in the informality, I was also aware of wanting something more from our meetings. The lightheartedness seemed to go hand in hand with a lack of depth and of content. I wanted our services to be meaningful – times when we would meet God.

Some of our members thought the answer lay in requiring more reverence, dignity and solemnity in the meetings. For others of us, common sense pointed to the rightness of being informal, especially in our district, but still we questioned it.

Typical of the questions in our minds at that time was whether the workers should call me 'Mr Brown', 'Chris' or 'Pastor'. It was not thought proper that I should be called 'Chris'. But I was not committed to the formality, and eventually 'Mr Brown' and 'Pastor' were dropped as titles.

It was also thought that Sue should be called Mrs Brown, but they found that hard right from the beginning!

A radical step?

In May 1970 I took what we all thought was a very radical step: I started a morning family service for the Christians who lived in the area.

Here, at least, we could be free from unnecessary traditions. We used a small side-room furnished with armchairs. In a corner stood a table supplied with drawing implements for the children to use during the message. We numbered twelve adults and six children.

The meeting was still led from the front but included an 'open time', when anyone could share needs, experiences or answers to prayer. It was another step in the direction of the teaching, fellowship, breaking of bread and prayers of Acts 2. I had read about the 'experience meetings' of the early Methodists and they seemed a good idea. So we included fellowship as part of the service, rather than just something for afterwards.

We certainly weren't copying any other group; we didn't know of any others who were doing the same thing at that time. We enjoyed the meetings. They were refreshingly different. Also, as new people started coming to us, we seemed to be making progress.

Treadmill of activity

If we were radical in some things we were definitely not in others.

We were trying to keep up the same number of activities as other churches who had far more members. There were always constant demands on our time from the many needs which arose in the district. We were, for instance, the only people who owned a long ladder and I was at intervals asked to get through a window three or four floors up when a key had been forgotten.

'Could you help us to move a bed to Brixton? It'll just go in your minibus.'

Being good neighbours to hundreds of local people was impossible. We had to learn to say 'no'.

My routine responsibilities included the Sunday services (leading and preaching); an after-church fellowship time; a boys' Bible class on Sunday afternoons, with its associated mid-week club; the mid-week prayer and Bible study meetings; visiting; support to the medical staff and visiting some patients; driving the minibus to fetch ladies for the women's meeting and then frequently being asked to speak to them; helping with the teenagers' club; organising and leading door-to-door evangelism; arranging evangelistic films and literature; acting as caretaker for the building; and being a husband and father.

Sue ran a young wives' group, helped in the girls' Bible class, took medical calls outside surgery hours, ran a home, coped with frequent callers, looked after the children and propped me up. Whew!

The many local needs that Lansdowne was still trying to meet meant that we were constantly overstretched and not doing any one thing effectively. At the time, we were proud of this treadmill of activity. We would take the opposite view now, but we didn't know anything different then.

We did a little work directly with adults through the women's meetings and the medical work. Every year hundreds of patients visited the doctor, who was sometimes able to suggest a visit from the pastor. My most fruitful work at that time was with some terminally ill people. It was lovely to see them find real peace and trust in Jesus before they died.

Dr Oxford and Nurse Turner were able to share a little of the gospel with patients, many of whom appreciated the love and care they received. But though the potential for the gospel was great – when people are in need they often cry out to God – we never seemed able to exploit it.

Had we seen many converts at that time, it is doubtful whether we could have held them. A friend from another church said, 'All our evangelism is like an arm beckoning,

''Come'', but there is no body to come to.' It was true. Christ's body at Lansdowne still seemed a long way from our New Testament vision.

One of our problems was a lack of unity. The 'us and them' mentality, so obvious in the district at large, also plagued the Mission people. Some local Christians accepted a two-tiered Christianity. In their thinking they were the lower class. The top class was reserved for the better-educated Christians, whom they assumed to be more spiritual. They just couldn't grasp the fact that they themselves were equally important to God.

This lie of the enemy impeded their growth and created misunderstandings, division and a lack of love. I didn't know how to combat the problem, except to teach them otherwise. My efforts, however, seemed to have little effect. The differences seemed doomed to defeat us.

We had better hopes for the young people and expected them to be different under our influence. But, sadly, the same seeds of inferiority were in their lives, too, and produced choking weeds later on.

A baptism!

Then – joy of joys! – one young lady asked for baptism. Now we were really on the verge of making it! She was the first baptismal candidate for years.

The occasion proved memorable. Not having a baptistry ourselves, I asked our local Baptist church if we could use theirs. Yes, they would be delighted, but as it hadn't been used for years they would have to make sure that the geyser supplying the hot water still worked. The geyser was duly tested and the okay given.

In due course we arrived at the church, where a frantic scene met our eyes. Ladies were scurrying to and from the kitchen with kettles and saucepans of hot water, emptying them into the baptistry, where it looked as if the tide had gone out! The geyser had refused to function once the first gallon of water had reduced the water pressure.

Sue, somewhat embarrassed, had her work cut out trying to allay the mother's anxiety.

'She isn't going to be baptised in that, is she? She'll catch her death of cold!' Then, at intervals during the service: 'That water's getting colder' – and similar comments.

Fortunately, the baptismal candidate was very petite and it was possible to dunk her fairly easily in a level of water which didn't even reach my knees. The great thing was, we'd had a baptism! 'More will follow,' we now thought. 'We're really getting somewhere.'

The bubble bursts

It was in 1972 that our bubble burst. Nearly all the young people on whom we had pinned our hopes began to drift. They represented years of work to us personally, and to others.

There were also rumbles of dissatisfaction on all sides. The lack of unity was becoming more obvious and was crippling us. We had disappointments with a lot of people. As soon as we had picked ourselves up from one let-down, something else would come and knock us over. We felt frustrated and lonely.

A report written around that time said, 'For those engaged in the work of the Lord at Lansdowne, this year has not been an easy one.'

That was an understatement. Sue and I were devastated. All we had built up was coming to nothing. Everything we had sacrificed in order to make our home in the inner city seemed wasted. We had failed – we who had been so sure of God's calling, so sure that we could succeed where others had failed. A handful of mission workers stuck with us faithfully, sharing our vision – and our frustration.

Looking back, I am sad about those young people, nearly all of whom left us and went back into the world. Obviously I was very upset at the time, too, but it came as a shock to realise *why* I was so upset. I was grieving, not because the Lord's work was coming to an end, but because I personally had failed. I was sorry for myself. My work had come to nothing, my pride was hurt.

It hit me hard to realise that, for all my good works, I was still a sinner. I had taken the Lord's work and made it my own. I had fancied myself to be a good servant to him, but I had really been serving myself.

I am profoundly grateful for the experience because it brought me to the end of myself and led me to a repentance beyond anything I had previously known. It marked a turning-point in my life and ministry. I thank God for my failure. Because of it, I cast myself on him as never before.

God's call confirmed

Sue and I both desperately wanted to leave. Our whole sense of call was in question. Did God still want us here? Was anything going to be retrieved from this mess?

Sometimes we would comfort ourselves by realising that we were a support to some individuals; our being there was an encouragement to them. But, beyond that, we didn't feel we were serving any useful purpose by staying.

Nevertheless, every time we considered leaving, God's call was confirmed again and again in reply to our doubts and questions.

On one such occasion I came home with an application form for a job as a probation officer. Normally Sue would have talked me out of it but this time she thought that maybe I was right. Maybe this work was no longer for me. Perhaps I would be more use serving the community in a different way. She opened her Bible and the words jumped out at her: 'God's gifts and his call are irrevocable.'

Sue didn't remember having read those words at all before that. I tore up the application form – God clearly wanted us to stay.

But we still didn't know what else we could do to bring

about our vision of seeing a New Testament church established in Bermondsey. I began to concoct various schemes for evangelism. We would go on trying the only way we knew.

But God had other plans. It was about this time that we were visited by a missionary friend, who preached into our situation. I was struck by it because never before had I heard anyone speak so directly to us as a body. He applied to us the story of Gideon – very specifically. To a man of faith, he said, the large numbers of those in opposition were no problem. We were few and surrounded by a host of enemies, but if we obeyed God in faith we would be bound to succeed.

I remember being puzzled. Hadn't we obeyed? Why then were we not seeing the blessing? It didn't add up.

Looking back, I realise that I knew how to obey God's word in general but knew nothing about hearing God's word for the details.

God prods

One day I came home after some door-to-door visiting and flopped down wearily in a chair.

'It's no good,' I said to Sue. 'No-one will ever believe the gospel the way I tell it. I wouldn't believe it myself, I'm so apologetic. The Bible says that the apostles spoke the word of God with boldness.'

In spite of all my good Bible teaching I was becoming aware that something was missing. My diary entry for 27 June 1972 reads: 'I feel the need for something extra in the work but I'm not able to say what.'

Around the same time we started to hear about charismatic renewal. An old school friend of Sue's wrote to us and we were amazed at the sense of life and joy which the letter conveyed. The last time we had seen her we had been very concerned for her spiritually depressed condition. Now she sounded like a new person. She told us about her baptism in the Holy Spirit and of her mother's healing from depression.

We were glad God had blessed her, even though we didn't think her terminology right. Like Gamaliel in Acts, we would see if it lasted.

'Lord, if there's anything else you want us to have, please show us,' we prayed. Though I prayed with sincerity, I remember also thinking, 'I don't think there is.'

I arrogantly thought that Pentecostals were a bit way-out and wild and that charismatics were superspiritual Christians, mainly in Anglican churches, who were more mystical than biblical. To my mind, the evangelical free churches of my upbringing were far more balanced. They seemed to be closer in line with the Word of God.

Sue had never been quite so convinced. Not having received as much Bible teaching as I had, she was not quite so blinkered and didn't assume the evangelicals had all the answers. She frequently asked me awkward questions.

'In the New Testament, the Holy Spirit told Philip to go and join the Ethiopian eunuch's chariot. Why don't we hear the Spirit speaking to us like that today?'

'Why don't we see people healed like the New Testament church did?'

I used to give my best, rational, theological answers.

Then one Sunday morning a young couple who had been worshipping with us for some time arrived very bright and full of life. They were almost bubbly – a sharp contrast to their normally quiet and shy selves. During our open time they told us of their experience of being filled with God's Spirit the previous evening.

I couldn't tie up the theology but the evidence was staring us in the face. They were unquestionably bolder, and full of joy. Affairs in the Mission, meanwhile, continued to go from bad to worse.

Then the leaders met together one evening. I intended to present my future plans for evangelism. We normally started with a short Scripture reading and prayer but, to my surprise, one of the leaders, who normally left the 'spiritual side' to others, asked if he could start off.

'I've been reading a book called *Nine O'clock in the Morning,*' he announced. 'I've read through Acts and have underlined all the references to the Holy Spirit. Is this what Lansdowne needs?'

Now I knew without a doubt what God was saying. My diary reads: 'Practical suggestions on evangelism dismissed. Only by the power of the Holy Spirit can anything be done.'

Gift of God's Spirit

The following week I attended a renewal meeting in Central London. I had previously thought of going but hadn't wanted to take time away from all our activities. Now I knew I had to go and that God was going to fill me with his Spirit.

I remember the meeting. It was nothing remarkable. Only a few people raised their arms while singing and the preaching was disappointing. I recalled on one occasion having been so gripped by Billy Graham's preaching that I had got up and gone forward, even though I was already a Christian. This meeting was nothing like that and so, when an appeal was made for people to come forward if they wanted to be filled with the Holy Spirit, I just sat still.

Then the thought suddenly struck me: 'Aren't I here because the Lord told me I would be filled?' Rather self-consciously I went forward and sat down with a group of people being prayed for. Someone behind me started to speak in tongues and it sounded phoney.

Then God poured out his Spirit on me! It was an amazing experience. There was a rushing in my ears, my eyes were quivering, my throat and tongue seemed tied in a knot. At the same time I just felt full up with love and praise for the Lord. I was 'lost in wonder, love and praise', as the old hymn expresses it.

I didn't speak in tongues as some others did. I didn't say anything. I went out and caught a bus home. But I was singing inside and, the next day in my office, still full of joy,

I tried to speak in tongues and found I could. Sue says that her quiet, English gentleman changed dramatically. Singing in the mornings before breakfast, of all things! I was bolder, more confident and full of praise to God. It was great!

Sue herself had been baptised in God's Spirit years earlier but hadn't put a label on it. She gradually came more and more into the good of that experience.

I entitled this chapter 'The blessings of failure'. When God wants to do a work he doesn't put methods and principles first. His priorities are our life and relationship with him. He seems as much concerned about what he wants to do *in* us as what he wants to do *through* us. He loves us too much to allow us success in our work for him at the expense of our relationship with him.

Some Christian enterprises seem to succeed for a while, but if God isn't at the centre they will come to nothing. We praise him for our failures. He has picked us up from them and given us something deeper and more lasting.

4

No strength to deliver

The Sunday evening following my baptism in the Spirit I stood up to preach. The usual faces stared back at me. To them it was just another Sunday but I was expecting something dynamic to happen.

It was after Jesus had been filled with the Spirit that he began his ministry. After Pentecost, Peter preached and three thousand were added to the church in one day. I felt so confident. God was with me – I knew it as I had never known it before.

My subject was 'New Life in Christ', my text Romans 6:4. The people listened well, some perhaps with a little more attention than usual, but that was all. No-one rushed forward crying, 'What must I do to be saved?' They seemed content to get up, exchange a few pleasantries and go home. It was nice that a few made favourable comments about my preaching, but I had hoped for so much more.

The next few years in Bermondsey touched the limits of both excitement and frustration. Sue and I experienced great personal blessing and yet, at times, desperate heartache. We frequently thought we were on the edge of a breakthrough, but it never came. Time and time again we were excited because this one or that one seemed ready to fall into the kingdom, only to experience bitter disappointment when it didn't happen.

We didn't know what else to do to see God move in the district and in the Mission.

What had changed?

What, then, *had* changed after my baptism in the Spirit?

For a start, I had times of exhilarating joy. My personal time with God became a delight. It was as if the truths of Scripture were now in full colour instead of black and white. Phrases which had been an enigma to me I now understood – phrases like: 'God has poured out his love into our hearts'; 'filled with inexpressible joy'; and 'the peace of God which passes understanding'.

Sorting out the doctrine was more of a problem because my experience didn't fit my previous understanding of the work of God's Spirit. I devoured every book on the subject I could find, including those which denied my experience. It took two years before I was satisfied and sure of what I would teach.

Baptism in God's Spirit should be experienced as an initial filling by God either at conversion or soon afterwards. God thereby equips his new child to be able to express love and worship to himself, to love others and to be a witness for him. It does not mean instant holiness. God continues to sanctify us throughout our lives.

Many Christians, like myself, have had to catch up on an experience which should have been ours from the beginning of our Christian lives. God's Spirit was promised as a result of Christ's work but I had not expected nor even asked God for baptism in the Spirit.

Fortunately for us all, he is full of grace. He continues to fill us again and again as we become thirsty and bring ourselves to him.

A weight lifted

The week following my being baptised in the Spirit, one of our Sunday school teachers came to tell me she had a non-Christian boyfriend and was resigning. A short while previously the news would have made me extremely depressed – this girl was a home-grown Christian, one of our successes.

I remember listening to her and being amazed that I was still singing inside! What was happening? Didn't I care any more?

A note in my diary reads: 'Was beginning to be content with the situation – was prepared to let Lansdowne die. Felt the need for urgent prayer.'

Another entry says: 'Feeling no longer able to cope with the work here. It is up to the Lord whether he blesses or not. Is this faith or laziness?'

God was underlining to me again the fact that only he could do it. It was his work, not mine. This realisation gave me a new freedom and relaxation in what I did. I gave up. I no longer thought that my own efforts would achieve anything.

Sue was getting the same message. One day she was vacuuming the front room. It was being done vigorously because she was angry.

'Lord,' she complained, 'you've called us here, but nothing's happening! How are the people out there going to believe when your church is in this mess? Don't you care about your glory?'

The Lord's voice came clearly, unmistakably, almost audibly: 'It's my church.'

The effect was instant. The weight rolled off her shoulders. His firm, gentle rebuke communicated his personal love and his overall control. Sue didn't need to know all the answers; she did need the Lord. He had come so refreshingly, giving a new realisation of his love for her as an individual as well as a knowledge that he was working out his larger purposes.

God was helping us to rely on him completely. We had failed but we had a new peace, even though we didn't have any new answers for the church.

Everything was to stem from our relationship with him. He would show us when to be burdened in prayer above our everyday prayers. He would direct our actions. If he said that our work was coming to an end we would accept it.

Exciting opportunities

New opportunities were opening up with adults. This seemed to be another result of my baptism in the Spirit.

By this time Sue and I and our children were better known and more accepted by the people in the district. They began to come to us with their problems and drew from us Christ's compassion. He gave us a love for them. In our naivety we tried to help them all, even though many of the problems were new to us.

Certainly it was stimulating. There were those involved in crime. There were drug addicts and alcoholics. I became accustomed to visiting prisons and the local magistrates' court.

Our door was always open to people and some came to talk with Sue about family problems. One girl came to confide about an unwanted pregnancy, another was scared to go home after running away. We learned to deal with con-men who came asking for money. Our older children learned to cope with school friends whose homes were being ruined because of alcoholism, strife or a lack of love and care.

I had a certain amount of experience of life in the raw but I was repeatedly shocked by what seemed an amoral society. These people's consciences had been seared 'as with a hot iron'. Some knew nothing of love or loyalty. They lived a hand-to-mouth existence, not only financially but also emotionally and socially. For many, violence was normal.

The funny side

Life was interesting, never boring and we were often amused, in spite of the hair-raising circumstances. It wasn't unusual to receive a telephone call from the police.

'We've got a friend of yours here at the station. We caught

him climbing over the wall out of Knightsbridge Barracks, having pinched a ceremonial sword from the Horse Guards. He's a bit the worse for wear. Can you come and fetch him?'

'We've got a lady here who says you might help her with bail. She's being charged with grievous bodily harm.' We were amazed – she had appeared so quiet and gentle!

A violent row broke out one night and, as it involved one of our 'friends', I was called out to help. Some time after the police had driven away I still hadn't returned home and Sue became a bit worried. She telephoned the police for information.

'Oh, yes, Mrs Brown,' came the calm voice at the other end of the line. 'Your husband was coping very well so we left him to it!'

One Friday night we were awakened by a ring at the doorbell. We looked at the clock. It was four in the morning. We guessed it was an alcoholic friend who was staying with us until we could get him into a rehabilitation centre. He had been paid that day and the temptation of a pocketful of money had proved too much.

He knew the rules: he wasn't welcome in our home if he was drunk. It wouldn't be the first time we had left him to sleep on the grass outside the front door. I crawled back into bed ten minutes later saying to Sue, 'You're never going to believe me – I've let in two of them!' A sober young fellow with nowhere to sleep had brought our friend home because he had been unwisely showing off his hard-earned cash.

At five our baby woke. I peeped in at our guests. I was horrified to see the top bed of the double bunk, where they were asleep, balancing precariously on only two diagonal supports. Our drunken friend had dislodged it as he had heaved himself up on to it and now both men were fast asleep, blissfully unaware of their predicament. We decided against trying to wake them and, closing the door, left them until morning.

We awoke on another occasion to the sound of loud music

from a nearby flat. Someone was having a party.

'Lord, we desperately need some sleep. Please shut them up,' we prayed.

We had barely finished our petition when an argument broke out between two lots of neighbours living on a different landing in the same block. One man smashed the next door's kitchen windows with a chair. Someone called the police and within ten minutes all was quiet and peaceful, including the party flat. We resumed our sleep, thankful for the prompt answer to our prayer!

Hopes dashed

Sometimes we were full of hope for these folk we spent so much time trying to help. Some seemed to be responding to the gospel. Our alcoholic friend would do well for a week or two only to fall right down again. It was disappointing and frustrating. Didn't God have the power to save such people completely? Yes, we knew he did, but it wasn't happening.

Others were still coming to us. The telephone was ringing – at midnight. What emergency would it be this time?

'Hello, Chris. I'm just ringing to see how you and Sue and the kids are?'

The caller was on drugs and involved in petty crime. He kept very different hours from us and it never occurred to him that we might be in bed.

We had known him since his Sunday school days. He told me once, when he was in our youth club, that he could see I liked him, so he couldn't understand why I sometimes threw him out. He was the same in adult life. He respected us, knew we liked him, so why weren't we willing to go along with some of his underhand ways?

He asked me for a lift one day. He had to collect something from a friend who was in a pub, he said. I was more than a little angry when I realised that the 'something' was the contents of the till and I was the getaway driver! He didn't try that one on me again.

We learned not to give money to callers. Sometimes we gave food. Sometimes I drove men to a Salvation Army hostel for the night.

A man came to the door on one occasion. 'I'm a window cleaner and my van's out of petrol. Please could you lend me money to get some more?'

I grabbed an empty petrol can. 'I'll take you,' I said.

Once in our vehicle the fellow admitted it was a false story and he really wanted the money for drugs. I spent time talking to him and discovered that he had friends who had recently become Christians. He had visited them in their rehabilitation centre and could see it was working for them, though, sadly, he had concluded that it wasn't for him.

Where was God's power to change these lives?

'Well, some people even turned away from Jesus himself,' people consoled us.

Yes, that was true, but we weren't seeing *any* come through. These people were coming to us. They could see we loved and respected them. They were amazed at our peace and freedom to move around without fear. They had none of these things. Yet the enemy still seemed to be firmly in control of their lives.

It wasn't much better in the fellowship. A few had come back to God and our numbers were a little better, but there were problems we seemed powerless to deal with.

I came into the kitchen one day to see a lady rolling on the floor. It was my first encounter with demon possession. She had started coming to the fellowship and now she came for advice over whether to stay with her non-Christian boyfriend, the father of her three children. We could help her a little with that practical problem, but here she was now, manifesting a spiritual problem, and we didn't have a clue how to deal with it.

There were many conflicts within families. One Asian girl came to us and became a Christian. Her parents had come to Britain in order to give their children a good education but they then expected them to slot back into the family religion and traditions. The older children totally rebelled. Our Christian girl couldn't bear to see her parents hurt any more so she consented to an arranged marriage to a Sikh man and left us.

Sue had some evangelistic coffee mornings for young wives. The response was encouraging. The women came, listened and asked questions. Still no-one was converted. Sue was called 'my social worker' by one young mother, because she listened and helped her through a difficult time of her life. She knew the gospel but didn't respond.

At the point of birth

'This day is a day of distress and rebuke and disgrace, as when children come to the point of birth and there is no strength to deliver them.' So reads Isaiah 37:3.

Our first baby was born with the aid of forceps. Any mother who has been through a hard labour, only to find that no matter how hard she tries she just hasn't got the strength to give birth, will understand the extreme weariness and frustration. Isaiah's words became increasingly real to Sue and me in relation to spiritual birth.

We felt acutely the 'distress and rebuke and disgrace'. It was as if there was 'no strength to deliver'. Many seemed near but it came to nothing. We were so dependent on God who brings life.

We had been reading the book of Jeremiah. God told the prophet that he would preach but no-one would listen, and in obedience he plodded on with the message. How we identified with him! We were prepared to go on even though nothing seemed to be happening and though our natural instincts told us to give up.

We felt that the church at large was under God's judgment. Unless his Spirit visited us we had no hope. We could only cry to him for mercy and grace.

James O. Fraser, the great missionary to China, wrote, 'Though the conflict be keen, although defeat seems certain, though the battle should continue for hours, for days, for months, even for years, yet hold on, HOLD ON, for to such Jeremiah 1:19 is written, "They will fight against you, but they shall not prevail against you. For I am with you . . . to deliver you.""*

Like Fraser, we were to prove God's faithfulness in due course.

Bermondsey crusade

Something else happened in 1974 which made the lessons God was teaching sink deeper into us.

The year previously, a number of new pastors had come into the mission halls and churches in Bermondsey. Our links with these congregations became stronger and we experienced warm fellowship with them. Nearly all were small, struggling works and the hardness of the task made us cling together. We enjoyed joint prayer meetings and embarked on a programme of evangelism which culminated in a united campaign in 1974.

I was thrilled. With so many working together (as many as a hundred at one joint meeting) we could make an impact on the district. Every home in the Bermondsey and Rotherhithe area had been visited three times during the year with three specially prepared items of literature. Advertisements went up outside the churches and halls.

The campaign week arrived. The evangelists from the Movement for World Evangelisation joined with us and with those from the London City Mission. Schools and factories were visited and special meetings put on for children, young people and adults. We had prayed, given financially and been to special counselling classes.

In spite of all the effort only five new Christians were added to the twelve participating churches and missions.

'Why?' we asked yet again.

A friend gave the answer in a nutshell: 'God doesn't put

* Quoted in *Mountain Rain*, by Eileen Crossman, STL, 1984

new babies on gravestones; he puts them into warm, loving arms.'

God had given as many newborn as we could cope with. Our churches just weren't ready.

Conclusions

Looking back, the lessons are obvious to us. It was indeed 'a day of distress and rebuke and disgrace'. So many were on the edge of new life but our *churches* weren't right. God, looking for a spiritual house, was making sure our foundations were firm before building further.

I realise now how lonely I was in leadership. As a pastor, I was expected to be good at everything. Although they called me 'pastor', most of my flock gave me no authority to lead. The church at large at that time was built on a foundation of rule by committee and consensus, not on the revealed will of God.

When God wanted to lead the children of Israel out of Egypt he didn't shout down and tell them to form a committee to decide what to do. He called Moses and gave him specific instructions. It was Moses who gave prophetic direction to the people. He was God's gift of leadership to them.

The result was effective, even though it meant hard work for Moses: God mightily delivered them.

In my situation, though I felt frustrated, God had given me authority in my preaching and I was more confident in him. But many still didn't see the need to act on God's preached word.

'I didn't realise you wanted me to do anything. I thought you were just preaching,' replied one young man when I asked him what he had done in response to the previous week's teaching.

Others were perplexed at the change in me, uncertain of the repercussions. Some were very critical, others alarmed.

God still at work

It wouldn't be right to end this chapter without mentioning the positive things which were taking place.

God *was* at work. He was working on us, his people – imparting to us his vision for a different, dynamic church. Some Christians, like us, were hungry for God to move in their personal lives, not satisfied with the mediocrity which existed.

Throughout this very difficult time God began to link me up with others. Bert Barritt, Bob Cheeseman,* Richard Haydon-Knowell, John Houghton and other brothers in South London, were a few names which were later to mean a lot to Sue and me and the church.

God was slowly releasing me from my independence and opening me up to others. But I am going on too fast.

*currently on TSS committee '96!

5

Light at last

It was early in 1974. Lansdowne had reached its lowest ebb.

It certainly didn't feel like spring. In vain we looked for new buds and shoots on our tree. But God was slowly and surely making the sap rise which was soon to bring out a miracle of new life.

God did it. First of all he spoke very specifically through his Word, then he started adding new people to our fellowship. He then began linking us up more positively with other like-minded leaders and churches.

Over the following few years a whole series of very significant events took place. We seemed to be no longer just plodding, but running.

God speaks

'He has appointed me to build a temple for him . . . . Anyone of his people among you – may his God be with him, and let him go up to Jerusalem in Judah and build the temple of the Lord.'

This was my text for the first of a new series of messages from the book of Ezra. Early in that year, as I preached, it seemed as if a weight was being lifted from us. Spring seemed to be stirring. I was aware of God's presence in a new way.

At the time I knew nothing of 'restoration' teaching – only what God was teaching me through the Scriptures. Looking back, I can see that the Ezra series was prophetic. It set out the Lord's direction for us. I had always believed in God's written Word; now I was learning to exercise faith in a new way. God was quickening his Word to me in my situation.

During the first week of the following year I awoke in the night and found myself fully alert. God gave me this word from 2 Kings 19:29 (RSV): 'This shall be the sign for you: this year you shall eat what grows of itself, and in the second year what springs of the same; then in the third year sow, and reap, and plant vineyards, and eat their fruit.' The passage goes on to say that a remnant of the house of Judah will again take root below and bear fruit above.

It was very vivid; there was no mistaking the voice of the Lord. But what did it mean?

Sue and I studied the passage. Jerusalem was under siege. King Hezekiah was hard-pressed and cried to God. God answered him by giving a promise for the future. He would again be free to sow, plant vineyards and reap. In the meantime God would still provide food for them to eat.

We were amazed to find that Isaiah's version of the same story contains the words of Hezekiah: 'This is a day of distress and rebuke and disgrace, as when children come to the point of birth and there is no strength to deliver them.' What a parallel to our own situation! We may not have been physically under siege, but we certainly were spiritually.

We couldn't wait for the 'third year', when there would be greater freedom and fruitfulness. We shared it with some close friends at Lansdowne to encourage them.

'Can we last out that long?' ventured one, reflecting the extreme weariness she felt.

'What grows of itself'

Instead of decline, we began to see growth.

'Can I come to your church?' the lady was asking as she came through the door. We could hardly believe our ears. We had spent years asking people to come; now here was someone asking us!

She was a local person who as a child, forty years before, had been fostered by Christians. Since then they had faithfully prayed for her. That week she had attended their funeral service following their sudden death in a car accident. At last she had turned to God.

Another lady turned up to an Easter morning service. We knew her children well – they had been coming to Sunday school. I remembered talking to her on a previous occasion and she had seemed very bitter. As a single parent she had learned to cope with life by hardening herself.

Although we tried, we couldn't get close to her. But we noticed that each time she came to the services she looked more relaxed, and we wondered what was happening inside her. Eventually Sue managed to break through her shyness and she agreed to come round for coffee.

'Have you a Bible to read?' Sue asked as they chatted in our kitchen.

'Oh yes, I've read as far as Daniel and some of the New Testament,' she replied.

'Did you know that the Old Testament points forward to Jesus and that he died to forgive us and give us new life?'

At this point the lady began to cry. 'Yes,' she said, 'It's already happened to me.'

It was obviously a relief for her to confess it to someone. There was no doubt that God had saved her. Her neighbours remarked on the dramatic change in her life. She became radiant and full of joy. Gradually the Lord healed her past hurts and today she is still a loving member of God's family in Vineyard. Her life is a testimony to God's love and power. The only thing we did was to be there!

My diary records for November 1975: 'Eighteen adults attended morning service.' That was an encouraging increase. Then I was overjoyed when, after one communion service, spontaneous singing broke out.

At last, after long debate, a church membership was formed. It was a step forward.

Other streams flowing

While all these changes were slowly taking place at

Lansdowne, God was doing similar things with others. Since my baptism in the Spirit I had been continually looking for fellowship with those of like mind. God began to bring me into new relationships, some of which were to prove very significant in the future. One of these was with Bob Cheeseman.

I was very wary of Bob when I first knew him. At the meetings of evangelical pastors this Pentecostal brother would punctuate our nice quiet prayer times with a 'Praise the Lord' or 'Hallelujah'.

'Most off-putting and unnecessary,' I thought, as it cut across my staid English temperament.

Shortly afterwards, though, I recognised that this man at least would understand what God had done in filling me with his Spirit. We began to have fellowship together.

Bob was serving the Lord in the Elim Church in Bermondsey. He also had a full-time secular job in London. His small group of Christians stood out to us. They enjoyed a quality of spiritual life which we coveted for our own church. They were committed to the hilt and seemed altogether more alive than we were.

Fire from heaven

There were only a dozen or so of them, meeting in a dilapidated old building. As their area was scheduled for redevelopment, the central Elim body weren't supplying any more money for its upkeep, and it was rapidly deteriorating.

Bob and Mary, with their two children, lived at Forest Hill and commuted in. The church ran similar activities to those of Lansdowne but without the medical and social work. They had ninety children in their Sunday school when we first knew them.

They could write a story similar to ours – about the hard work of pioneering, of the battles with youngsters and the frustration of knowing they had the answer for needy people who didn't want to know.

Like us, they plodded on even though they saw so little fruit.

One night in 1975 a few of them were praying, asking God for direction. The odds seemed heavily stacked against them. 'Lord, show us whether or not to carry on here,' they prayed. 'If you want us to keep this place open we will do it, but if you want it to close we will do that. Show us what is right.'

The next day their building was gutted by fire! It was a relief that God had answered very specifically. There was no way now that Bob was going to carry on trying to run an Elim church in another building. Most of the members saw the wisdom of linking up with other churches in Bermondsey.

Bob and Mary, with helpers, carried on running the Sunday school from different buildings loaned for the purpose. Looking back, they can see how God used the children to keep them in Bermondsey. 'Otherwise I don't think I would have stayed,' commented Bob.

God had matters very clearly in hand. Earlier in 1975 Bob had led a series of Bible studies at Union Chapel.

'If ever you're looking for a new pastorate,' the trustees told him, 'would you consider coming here?'

Bob knew from God right then that one day he would become a full-time leader there. A short time after the fire the trustees approached him again. Bob made his position clear: 'I'm prepared to come, but I won't compromise my Pentecostal convictions.'

The trustees, at least, agreed that he could be himself and received him into leadership in November of the same year.

Fresh promise

At Bob's induction service the Lord spoke to the church from Isaiah 42:9: 'See, the former things have taken place, and new things I declare; before they spring into being I announce them to you.'

That verse was to crop up again and again in the following months. It was exciting.

The dozen or so people at Union Chapel at that time received their new pastor with mixed emotions. Bob was careful not to bulldoze in with his Pentecostal teaching, but he wasn't going to mark time either. These struggling servants of God needed the empowering of God's Spirit. They knew themselves to be at a low ebb.

Situated just near Tower Bridge, Union Chapel has a history going back more than two hundred years. It is very chequered – times of increase as well as decline, division among people, financial difficulties and wartime bomb strikes followed by rebuilding works. The foundation stone of the present building in Tooley Street was laid on 4 October 1958.

Only a few years prior to the opening of the new building, the pastor at the time had written: 'Never have we seen such loyalty and spiritual growth as we witness in our young people today, which indeed speaks well for the future of the church, since it is to these young people that we look to carry on the work which is so dear to us.'

Where were those people in 1975? Not in Union Chapel. It had been so discouraging for the members to see all but two fall away or move out of the district. Now, with a new pastor, maybe things would pick up again.

One of the ladies, now in her seventies, was in Union Chapel when Bob started.

'I had a terrific struggle with Bob's teaching,' she recalls, 'but I wouldn't go back now. I've followed Bob rather begrudgingly at times, but God has blessed me through him.'

Soon after Bob started, things began to pick up. Some people working with the London City Mission's Voluntary Evangelism Scheme started coming to Union Chapel. Then another older couple. Then, joy of joys, a couple were converted.

'Like a desert land with two new shoots coming up,' someone described it.

While these additions were encouraging, Bob remained far

from satisfied. 'Please, God, do something,' was his constant, desperate plea.

Some of his flock were responding to his teaching but many were still not baptised in the Spirit. Some left.

'I will do a new thing,' God had promised. At times it was hard to stick with it.

It was no wonder that Bob and I had a lot to talk about. Our friendship deepened. In July 1976 I invited him to preach at Lansdowne. Gradually our two fellowships joined together for other times of fellowship. A watchnight service at the end of the year, baptism services and eventually some united Sunday evening meetings when the Deaf Christian Fellowship, led by Bert Barritt from Rotherhithe, also joined us.

Other links

The London City Mission (LCM) had a mobile evangelistic unit and in late 1976 and early 1977 they came to help us at Lansdowne, organising door-to-door visiting, films and open-air sessions. Some of the young voluntary evangelists also came – young people who gave up a year of their time to serve God in evangelism with LCM.

Two of them were David Nunn and Lesley Norcross.

'We liked working with Lansdowne,' Lesley remembers. 'There was an incredible spirit about the evangelism we did there. Christians from the fellowship came and joined with us. There was a warm family atmosphere about the place and people were alive. We felt it was worth inviting people to. The mobile unit leaders felt the same.'

In March 1977 Lesley had a vision from God.

'There was a huge wheel of fire. As it rolled down Abbey Street, smaller wheels were shooting from it, rolling along the smaller streets and then up the staircases into the blocks of flats. I was so excited. God was going to do something great.'

God's promise confirmed

LCM asked local pastors to go and give Bible studies to the voluntary evangelists. In January that year, after I had finished one of these studies, a young man handed me an envelope.

'God gave me these verses for you when I was praying last week. At first I thought it was just me wanting to encourage you, but this morning I read the same verses where they are repeated in Isaiah. I knew then that they were from God.'

I opened the envelope and on the single sheet of paper was written a reference: 2 Kings 19:29, 34. Our hearts leapt with fresh joy as Sue and I turned again to the words God had given me (v29) almost exactly one year previously. Verse 34 was added: 'I will defend this city to save it, for my sake and for the sake of David my servant.'

'The city of God' was a phrase which was taking on new meaning for us. It referred to the people of God together, the church, not to a place in the Middle East.

Jesus' words, 'I will build my church', began to come alive for us. The church had its origin in God. Jesus as its Head was alone its source of life. The birth of the church was a miraculous act which only God could perform. He would save it for the sake of Jesus, David's greater Son.

Our efforts to plant and build were useless unless God's Spirit was present. Many times Christians have taken hold of the church and made it theirs, without relying on God's help. They have dictated how it should be run and organised, thought of 'better' ways to do things, often without being tuned in to its Author and Finisher.

God began to forge other links with some pastors from Catford and South Lee. I had known Richard Haydon-Knowell for many years and our paths had crossed from time to time. He invited me to join with the South London pastors' meetings.

It was there that I, and later Bob, found the fellowship we had been looking for. God had been speaking to these men and to us on the same themes. How refreshing it was to be free to talk and share together.

'Tell my people they have to change'

In April 1977 I took the step of inviting Richard Haydon-Knowell to speak at a special weekend we were having at Lansdowne. I knew he would bring definite direction, and he did: God was saying to us, 'Tell my people that they have to change. I am an unchanging God but there can be no improvement without change.'

It was a clear word. We responded to God, asking him to change us and our situation. It was a costly decision.

About that time I went home one day to talk over something with Sue. She thought I was mad. Sue says, 'We'd often thought about buying a tent and going camping, but now Chris was going to do it! Now, when I was pregnant with our fifth child. Now, when I had more than ever to cope with. The baby would be three months old in August when he proposed we should go to the Dales Bible Week! My heart failed me.'

Apart from the inevitable hard work, Sue had reservations about that charismatic crowd. She wasn't at all sure she wanted to go to the Bible Week.

'I knew from the way Chris was talking that God had spoken to him. I agreed to go but had mixed feelings. On the one hand I was nervous but, on the other, I didn't want to miss out on what God was doing.'

Bob and I were certain God wanted our two families there. Together with two close friends from Bermondsey we began to make preparations. Bert and Marie Barritt were also going with some deaf Christians.

As Sue and I were usually exhausted when we first arrived on holiday, I reasoned that if we took a break first we would go to the Dales Week fresh. So it was that at the end of July we stayed in a friend's cottage in an idyllic part of Wales. It should have been lovely but the holiday wasn't one of our best.

The weather was poor, with low cloud covering us nearly all the time. Post-natal blues had hit Sue and the short break didn't revive her sapped energy.

As we drove across country to Yorkshire the day was unbearably hot. Two of our children were travel sick. We arrived tired and irritable. The large sign proclaiming 'Jesus Welcomes You' seemed presumptuous and the cheerful people waiting to hug us at the check-in superficial. All we wanted to do was find a quiet corner and be forgotten. But there was no hope of that among these thousands of people!

The first meeting made me realise this was going to take some getting used to. It was all so big, the worship was so noisy and not being in a church party we felt isolated. Bob and Mary, having originated from the Pentecostal movement, didn't have quite such a shock but even they were a bit intimidated by the size of the thing.

Sue was shocked, when she peeped into one of the children's meetings, to see them dancing as part of their worship. It just didn't seem right to her.

But our children loved it. The week had a particular effect on our nine-year-old. He had never enjoyed being in London and that year he had been very depressed at times. It wasn't the first time, or the last, that we had thought of moving out of the city for his sake.

On the Thursday evening he came back from his meeting so happy that he couldn't stop singing. He woke early the next morning still singing. There was no doubt that God had touched his life. It was great to see him free of the depression. Sue realised it was all from God.

The week was outstanding. We had a real sense of destiny – we were meant to be there. Bert, Bob and myself were constantly marvelling at how God was piecing everything together. Mary, Sue, Marie and our two friends shared the excitement. The things God had revealed to us in our own situation, he had also revealed to more people than we had imagined. We learned so much; it was a turning-point.

Aftermath

'What shall we say? How much shall we tell them?' These were our thoughts as we drove back down the M1 towards London.

We were full up with all that we had seen and heard. Normally when we drove towards London it was with an attitude of grim determination, but this time we could hardly wait to get back. What, though, would we tell people? How were they going to react? We decided to go easy at first and reveal more as they asked questions.

We had been home only a short time when a friend called to welcome us back. Our children ran up to her, still very excited.

'Do you know what happened?' they cried. 'Some people saw some angels!'

Our poor friend was very polite but, not surprisingly, didn't know how to respond. Our plans for caution were thrown to the wind. Over the next few weeks we told them about the worship, the singing in tongues, the tremendous preaching and the healings.

'I thought you'd been to heaven,' remarked one lady. 'You all look so radiant.'

What had we come away with? Was it just froth and bubble, as some Christians suggested? Would it wear off in a short time? If there was froth and bubble it was because God himself had put some 'fizz' into our faith. He had given us new zest and powerfully changed our lives.

For Union Chapel, the Deaf Christian Fellowship and Lansdowne this was a turning-point. Things would never be the same again.

New understanding

In retrospect, we can see clearly some of the lessons we learned at that time.

We saw that 'The earth is the Lord's.' Oh yes, we had

known it before, but now we realised that it also meant, 'Bermondsey is the Lord's.' Subconsciously we had always viewed the city as the enemy's territory. Now we saw that Satan's activity is only a temporary incursion. He is trespassing on God's ground. We knew now that God was going to triumph in our area and that knowledge increased our faith.

Our vision of the church was strengthened and clarified. We could see what it really meant to be 'built together to become a dwelling in which God lives by his Spirit' (Ephesians 2:22).

Worship now had a clearer meaning. The hymn-prayer sandwich had already started to go. I now sought to lead the people into worship which was led by God's Spirit, giving him freedom to express his gifts through us.

It was one thing to raise my hands with several thousand others but now I had to learn to lead my own people. I took up a tambourine and danced because I wanted to express my joy to God. But being aware of the opinions of some who watched, I didn't find it easy.

We were not just looking for change, though, nor even informality. We were looking for freedom in worship so that we could follow the promptings of God's Spirit. We didn't want to break old, traditional habits merely to establish new ones. We wanted to base what we did on Scripture.

I spent time with those who were not happy, explaining why I was doing things. It was all very painful for me and for them. I wanted to understand and care for them but they saw what I was doing as divisive. They were afraid we were just following a movement, that we were 'over the top'.

I searched my own heart, but always I came back to the fact that I must follow God's leading. He must come first. I constantly prayed that everyone would understand and follow as well.

Was it fair on the fellowship for me to carry on? After all, I had changed under a powerful spiritual experience and I was very different from the man they had first called as their pastor. I offered to stand down. I couldn't compromise on God's leading but they must choose whether or not they still wanted me.

I stayed. Although many didn't understand, they could see that I was there because God had put me there.

No uncommanded work

Anything that got in the way of our 'building a spiritual house' must go. There were always so many needs in the inner city, all clamouring for attention. Sometimes I felt like a juggler trying to keep plates spinning on poles. When the youth work started to run down I rushed over to give it a bit more impetus. When I noticed the evangelism needed a boost, over I would rush to that. It was a constant battle to keep it all up.

Then a phrase hit us between the eyes: 'Do no uncommanded work.'

I knew this was God's word to me. He had given me a pastoral and teaching gift. If I neglected to use his gifts by focusing on other tasks, I was failing him. My job was to do what he told me to do. The youth work, the many evangelistic activities, the open Sunday school all had to go. God had told us to build him a spiritual house. We must get that house in order first.

Bert, Bob and I knew that God had joined us together in a special way. We had never known such unity before. Ephesians 4:16 talks about the whole body being joined together under Christ. We were the 'bones' next to each other.

'Bones meeting' entries appeared in our diaries as frequently as Bert's schedule permitted. They were 'glory times'. We had total freedom and confidence with each other. We were all learners ready and eager to get going. The times were punctuated by shouts of praise, singing and laughter.

The promise underlined

It was January 1978. I was in one of the Bermondsey united church prayer meetings along with others from the fellowship. One of the church leaders was reading from 2 Kings 19. Yes, you've guessed! 'This year you will eat what grows by itself, and the second year what springs from that. But in the third year sow and reap, plant vineyards and eat their fruit.'

The person reading didn't know the significance those words had held for us. This was the 'third year'. God had meant it literally. I felt free to forge ahead. Bob, Bert and I arranged a series of prayer meetings for those in our three fellowships who wanted to pray for the work of God's Spirit.

About thirty people crowded into our large front room. 'Bones and flesh' was entered into our diaries. We were able to worship God freely, uninhibited in praying in tongues, voicing prophecy and singing worship songs.

It was the start of new growth. 'Instead of the thornbush will grow the pine tree, and instead of briers the myrtle will grow.'

Our 'Jeremiah' days were over. We were thrilled with God, caught up with a sense of destiny, of being involved with his miracle.

6

Which way forward?

As I was walking in the countryside one day, I noticed an old tree stump. Out of its centre grew a healthy young sapling.

It was a lesson to me. The new life at Lansdowne was like the sapling. As the new tree grew, the old, dead stump would give way. I wouldn't need to take an axe to the old wood, thereby risking damage to the new. I must concentrate on nurturing the new.

My only desire was to follow God. I had no wish to hurt people and cause controversy – but I found myself accused of both. On the one hand, we were experiencing great blessing, with increased unity, love and purpose. On the other, we were the cause of concern, fear and suspicion. It was heartbreaking. It threw us back again and again on God, who constantly confirmed that we were on the right path.

The stir-up was widespread in other churches. Many Christians who wanted to be Bible-based were asking the question, 'Is this of God or the enemy?'

The radical nature of what was being taught by Christians like those from the Dales Bible Week produced strong reactions. Many comments and judgments were made:

'Beware the three E's: error, emotionalism and exclusivism.'

'Emotionalism is dangerous; people will get carried along by the euphoria and be swept into error.'

'Surely tongues were only for New Testament times; we don't need them now.'

'You're being taken over by a movement.'

'The teaching on authority is dangerous – best leave it alone.'

Arguing with God?

I well understood. I'd faced many such questions in myself.

Some of the discussions and books which have debated the issues raised by 'restoration' teaching have been very theoretical, as if the way of God could be discovered by a rational process. But it isn't so simple. I believe God leads *in life* from where we are at a given time, and he does it by revelation of his will.

We didn't discover new ideas; they discovered us. We soon saw that they were rooted firmly in God. They were there plainly in Scripture and we were excited to find them. They were there for our benefit and guidance.

At times I tried to back off from this teaching, which was radical and costly. I questioned it from a distance but I found myself arguing with God himself.

Perhaps you can identify with me in this. You listen to a preacher and think of a whole series of reasons why he might be wrong. You suddenly find that you are arguing with God over something he is bringing to your attention at the time. He alone sees everything perfectly. Subsequent experience proves the rightness of the direction he gives.

I, and others with me, witnessed the truth of 'restoration' teaching. It is our testimony that the blessing we have seen since then in this inner-city church stems largely from it. I had been told that Pentecostals and charismatics were weak on doctrine. It wasn't true of those I was mixing with.

We were hungry for more, and when a series of 'celebration meetings' was arranged for the Lewisham area in South-east London we waited eagerly for each one. We read *Restoration* magazine from cover to cover, then bought back-numbers to catch up on previous teaching.

Is it biblical?

The themes were taken up in our Bible studies and discussions. They included discipleship, authority, community life, worship, grace and law, the kingdom of God, prophesying, family life, body ministry and church foundations. Previously we had concentrated largely on gospel preaching, doctrine and personal holiness.

Some of the relevant scriptures we had read before but either hadn't really noticed their truth or hadn't thought they could be applied and put into practice.

'You're always preaching about baptism in the Spirit,' complained one Christian.

It wasn't strictly true, but when a biblical teaching has been forgotten it needs more time given to it in order to emphasise its importance. A bit like a craftsman who, finding his pupil weak in a particular area, will take time to go back over the ground until the area becomes part of the whole, blending in with the rest.

'Is it biblical?' is a question I was constantly asking myself. Some time previously I had gained much from Dr Martyn Lloyd-Jones' book on Ephesians 2. The second part of his book, dealing with God's plans for the church, had particularly excited me. I now felt I was learning how to put the teaching into practice.

Fear of further links

Bob, Bert and I had felt joined together by God at the Bible Week in 1977. Now we were being drawn to link up in fellowship with brothers in the Lewisham area and with Terry Virgo on the south coast.

We had our doubts. We felt that Bermondsey was so different from the places where these brothers worked. Could someone from Hove really understand about life in Bermondsey? Our commitment to the local church had made us parochial and introspective. This is always a danger but the special needs of the inner city made us doubly so.

In any case, I firmly believed that the powerless inner-city churches, above all, needed to be self-governing. I didn't want to put us in a position of being taken over by others. Only recently the Mission council had been disbanded at Lansdowne – we no longer needed men from outside to make decisions for us.

My fears were groundless. I saw that these new brothers were concerned with the *principles* of church-building. There was plenty of room for local variations of practice.

I saw, too, that they did us good. They were further life-links. Like our flocks, we pastors needed care from others. We learned to receive from these men, and it strengthened us all in every way. It also released us from our isolation.

Another of my fears had been that we would be carried along with this new group only to find that, after its initial blossoming, it would become just another denomination littering church history.

It is not possible to legislate for the future. Our responsibility, we realised, is always to follow God's leading now. What Jonathan Edwards wrote back in the eighteenth century is still true: 'The task of every generation is to discover in which direction the Sovereign Redeemer is moving and then move in that direction.'

Prophetic teaching was being given to our generation concerning the church. It was the answer to all our longings to see the church established on a right foundation. The 'restoration' churches, as they were later known, were full of life and based on God's Word. That's what we wanted. We would move in the direction God was moving.

A definite step

Bob, Bert and I decided to make contact with John Houghton from South Lee early in 1978. He in turn related to Terry Virgo. We spent time with John, talking over our ideas and programmes and specific pastoral problems. He proved to be committed to us and honest with us.

'Don't you think you're trying to do too much too soon?' he questioned over one matter, or, 'Do you believe this is God's direction or is it just your own idea? If it's of God, then push through.'

Never did he impose on us or dictate what we should do. In no way were we being 'taken over'. Terry Virgo was the same. We all met up together some time later to establish our relationship. We found Terry to be a man of God with a heart for the kingdom, fully committed to the Scriptures and to moving with God. We trusted him. He was God's man for us.

Apostles and prophets – today?

He pointed out to us the need for the five-fold ministry gifts of Ephesians 4:11-12: 'It was [Christ] who gave some to be apostles, some to be prophets, some to be evangelists and some to be pastors and teachers, to prepare God's people for works of service, so that the body of Christ may be built up until we all reach unity in the faith.'

When these five ministries operated, they equipped each local church to function with the full breadth of God's working. In addition, each Christian was free to operate in such manifestations of the Spirit as words of wisdom, words of knowledge, faith, healing, miraculous powers, prophecy, the ability to distinguish between spirits, tongues and the interpretation of tongues (see 1 Corinthians 12:7-11).

I had been taught from the beginning that the church must be built on the foundation of the apostles and prophets. But I had given the truth a particular interpretation – the common view that these ministries belonged only to the New Testament period. They were the ones who laid down the foundation of the Scriptures for us to follow.

Was it right that Jesus was still giving apostles and prophets today? The very idea filled many Christians with horror. In their thinking, the apostles of the New Testament era had become semi-divine, and they expected their professed modern counterparts to add to the Scriptures.

We began to understand, however, that there were apostles in the New Testament besides the Twelve and that Christ continues giving such apostles and prophets 'until we all reach unity in the faith'. Modern apostles were not setting out to contradict the Scriptures, let alone add to them. If they did, we wouldn't have anything more to do with them.

At first, we cautiously said, 'Terry has apostolic gifting.' Later, we acknowledged him as an apostle, a gift given by God to his church, and John Houghton as a prophet and teacher to us in our need.

Aims

Not surprisingly, all this began to have an impact on our churches. John asked us what our aims were for 1979. After prayer and discussion we felt our first priority was to see body ministry and open worship established. We wanted to get away from a one-man ministry.

'How many of you have ever been given prophecy from God?' John asked our combined fellowships when teaching on the gifts.

Only a few put up their hands, but that didn't reflect the true situation. Quite a lot more could have said yes, but people were looking for something superspiritual. We were becoming more aware that God could use all of us as we responded to the promptings of his Spirit.

Our early attempts at open worship were exciting and painful. Leaders were no longer putting God's teaching in a feeding-trough where folk could come and get it if they wanted it. A direct response was expected. Some weeks people responded well. At other times, when the meetings fell flat, we were tempted to go back to the hymn-prayer sandwich – it was so much safer and more straightforward.

After three months we had broken through. Inhibitions were crumbling and we were learning to move with God's Spirit.

Sadly, a few people left. This type of meeting wasn't for them. The last thing we had wanted was division. I remembered the picture of the stump and the sapling, which encouraged me, but it was still hard. These were people I loved. But I had to trust God for them and concentrate on the direction in which he was taking me.

Some of those who stayed found it all very difficult but didn't want to sever their life-link of love and loyalty. They were greatly blessed in the long run. Others came to join us, attracted by the life and warmth. After two years we were growing in spite of those who had left.

Differing views of 'church'

One local Christian was talking to an Assemblies of God member with whom she worked.

'I understand why *you* worship like you do, but why did the Browns have to change?' she wondered.

On the surface, the contention was over the different form of service we had adopted. But that wasn't the real issue. Behind it lay two different views of what 'church' was all about.

One view understood the church to be a *building* or *institution* (denomination) to which individual Christians belonged. The other view saw it as a *people* relating together under the care and direction of a 'shepherd', regardless of buildings or institutions. When the New Testament speaks of 'the church that meets in her house', it clearly means people – a local group of Christians.

Accordingly, we began to teach our people that *they* were the church.

The cricket match

At last Lansdowne, Union Chapel and the church of the deaf were apparently making progress. The unity, love and life seemed more like the New Testament church we aspired to. It was much more alive than it used to be. I remember thinking, 'Lansdowne's on its way at last.'

Then something happened to throw us into turmoil again. We had to learn that constant change was with us to stay. God never lets us settle and stagnate.

In June 1979 Bob and I went to a leaders' meeting at Haywards Heath. It was one of the many times when Bert was away attending to his work among the deaf. During the lunch break we took our sandwiches out to a local park and sat watching a cricket match. We have never forgotten it. It's not that the cricket itself was anything special, but the conversation that took place as we watched.

'What you and I really ought to be doing is working together,' said Bob. 'Our vision's the same, and our gifts are complementary.'

I agreed with him, but neither of us could see how it could happen. Should Bob leave Union Chapel and join himself and his people to Lansdowne? Should I leave Lansdowne? Could we realistically join the two groups? Where would we meet? It seemed impossible.

Guidance

The following week we met with John Houghton. His opening question was: 'Have you ever thought of joining your two churches together?'

We nearly fell off our chairs!

'We were only talking about it last week. We'd love to, but we can't see how.'

We shared our thoughts and all the obstacles. John's counsel was obviously from God – it answered our questions.

'You could carry on using both buildings. Form a new church under joint eldership, have a morning meeting at Union and an evening meeting at Lansdowne.'

As time went on, John thought, it would be clear which was the best building to use long-term. Our fellowship members would have to give up their links with a building and see themselves as a people. It wasn't going to be easy. It would involve a lot of time and effort.

We took the next three months to pray and plan. We

needed to be sure that it was from God and not just a good idea of ours. What were our goals? Who would be leaders? We would need a new constitution and a new name. Our concepts must be clear and be communicated clearly to our people.

We felt the weight of responsibility. In effect we were bringing the individual works to an end – years of history for both places. How would our people cope? They had been so loyal. Particularly at Lansdowne, a strong community involvement with the estates around us had been built up. Would we lose it?

We wrestled and prayed about every aspect of the proposed merger until, in our hearts, we became sure it was of God. So we had to agree to go ahead, and asked him to sort out the difficulties.

It wasn't until the autumn that we brought the issue before those who helped in leadership. The conviction was ours but they needed to see it for themselves and be willing to go with us.

We could see many good reasons for forming a single church. One was that we were very short of manpower. The Jews always said that at least ten men were needed to form a synagogue. At Lansdowne we had six, and Union had six. We saw, too, that in the New Testament there was plurality in leadership. We were still in the tradition of a 'one-man ministry' and we wanted to get into line. Our few young people would benefit from being with others. Older members would also gain from being in a larger fellowship.

We wanted an Acts-type church characterised by life, love, purity and power. A church having people committed fully to Christ, to their leaders and to each other, not isolated in independence but drawing on the apostolic and prophetic gifts of the wider church. Only then would we have an answer to the stranglehold which the powers of darkness had on our district.

Breaking things up?

The proposal came as a shock to our respective leaders. After many years of struggle at Lansdowne, we had come to a place of unity and growth. Church life was a joy to us all, the opponents of 'life in the Spirit' had left, we had come to a broader place. Now it looked as if I was proposing to break it all up.

For a further six months we prayed and discussed the issues. The difficulties were mostly practical and psychological. The Christians from both fellowships got to know each other more as we arranged joint meetings and activities.

Eventually we decided to bring the matter of joining to all the members. We still had a tradition of democracy – each person could vote on the issues raised. Bob and I took time to see each member individually and explained what the plans were. Then the day came, in March 1980, when each fellowship held a church meeting.

'This is the way I want to lead you. Will you come?' I asked our Lansdowne people.

Eleven said yes. The other twelve said no or abstained. I was shattered. The people had seemed to be with me. Where had I failed? What had gone wrong?

Basically, they were afraid. The consequence of making such a big decision was too much for them to cope with. Some felt that, while they could trust Bob and myself, they were unsure about input from outside.

'We don't really know this John Houghton and Terry Virgo,' they argued.

At the other meeting, all but two of Bob's people had voted in favour. He too was shattered by my result. I was in turmoil. Did the result mean that I would have to resign and go and join Bob? That would leave twelve people to carry on at Lansdowne. 'It all seems wrong,' I cried to God.

That night a friend was due to stay with us. He arrived straight from a meeting where he had been the speaker. Knowing nothing of my predicament, he spontaneously shared with Sue and me what he had been saying at his meeting. It was from the story of the Israelites. Because Moses had been so long up the mountain, the people had grown restless and Aaron had given in to their demands to make the golden calf, an idol they could worship.

Our friend drew from the story the folly of listening to the people when God had clearly shown the way. Aaron tried to keep everyone happy.

'Leaders must have the courage to lead from the front, not from the middle,' our friend concluded.

It was God's answer to me. I must go forward. I must trust God for the outcome. Sure enough, over the next week many of the local people who had voted against the merger contacted me.

'I've been convicted,' said one. 'I didn't want to join but God has shown me that that was my own way, not his. I'm sorry. I'll come with you.'

Others followed and, by the end of the week, only those who lived at a distance were not in agreement.

'We could never agree to such a proposal, but we can see that now's the time for us to find a church nearer our homes.' They bowed out graciously.

There was no reason for any further delay. The last weekend in May was to be the start of our new church.

7

The marriage

We were excited yet nervous, sure yet fearful, confident yet feeling vulnerable. Bob and I had taken on the responsibility of bringing two long-established works to an end. We now had to channel our people in a new direction. We felt out on a limb, going into unknown territory, totally thrown on God.

On Saturday 3 May 1980 we enjoyed a celebration meal, our 'marriage feast', and then broke bread together. We called ourselves Bermondsey Christian Fellowship (BCF), one body now instead of two groups. For a while the join would show but then gradually disappear.

We set out our main purpose: 'Our aim is to be an expression of unity in the body of Christ, given up to the praise and worship of our gracious God; seeking to establish the kingdom of God through the proclamation of the gospel of our Lord Jesus Christ in the power of the Holy Spirit.'

This statement was written in the front of the book in which all new members signed their names. We meant it. We still long to see it in increasing measure.

Enjoying God together

The next day we met together for our first services, in the morning at Union Chapel and in the evening at Lansdowne.

There was a new freedom to express our praise. It was great, a bit like when Sue and I and the children moved to a ground floor flat after living above the doctor's surgery: we didn't have to worry so much when the children made a bit more noise – apart from our own mental health!

In our worship we were now free to make mistakes. No-one

would get upset if we only had one hymn instead of four or if a song was started in the wrong key. We were all committed to working things out together in a positive way.

We encouraged our people to use whatever gifts they had. Some were very talented musically whereas others were not so good, but we set out to 'make a joyful noise to the Lord'.

Two of our teens, on finding a couple of old fifes in a cupboard at Union Chapel, cleaned them up and learned to use them. They were both delighted later on to acquire flutes by the generosity of others and both became quite accomplished.

So our range of musical instruments increased and together we enjoyed God in our meetings. We learned to meet each other's eye when singing songs like *Our God Reigns,* thereby exhorting and encouraging one another as we sang. We aimed to follow Paul's injunction to do 'everything decently and in order', not by formality and a set order of service but through our oversight as elders.

Covenant people

We were still seeking to follow the New Testament pattern.

'See how those Christians love one another,' is still the best witness to the world. 'All the believers were together and had everything in common . . . . Every day they continued to meet together in the temple courts. They broke bread in their homes and ate together with glad and sincere hearts, praising God and enjoying the favour of all the people. And the Lord added to their number daily those who were being saved' (Acts 2).

'Your church has such a high level of commitment,' commented an older lady who visited us for a time. Our city was crowded with lonely, isolated people and our church was an oasis in the desert for any who wanted to join with us.

We often talked of covenant relationship. Christians are all in the new covenant in Christ. It is a binding agreement made by God which he will not break. We are therefore bound with ties of love and loyalty to each other. Love for one another and fellowship together are important expressions of our individual fellowship with God in the one covenant.

Scripture exhorts pastors to shepherd the flock of God, underlining the importance of this by reminding the flock that their pastors 'must give an account' (Hebrews 13:17). Christians are therefore exhorted to 'obey your leaders and submit to their authority'.

As elders, Bob and I had full authority, given by God and acknowledged by the people. It gave us freedom to rule and give guidance under God's direction. We loved our people and they loved us. Sometimes we worried that they accepted our authority too easily, and we encouraged them to question and check with God the counsel we brought to them. We didn't want a naive acceptance of everything we said.

'My parents are worried that I've got involved with something like the Moonies,' one of our student nurses shared with us one day.

She was having difficulty reassuring them, so Sue and I arranged for them to come and see us. Naturally enough, they were very concerned for their daughter, living away from home. To them we sounded rather radical and community-orientated. Were we some strange sect?

We managed to put their minds at rest. Yes, we were radical, yes, we did have an emphasis on community and leadership, but each individual was fully respected. There was no way we wanted to take over their daughter. She was free to go if she wished.

Our student nurse chose to stay, catching the vision and settling locally, throwing her energies into the life of the church. There are many like her.

Heavy authority?

A young man was courting a girl from our church.

'Will you marry me?' he asked her.

'I'd like to chat it over with my pastor first,' came her reply.

Her would-be husband was horrified. What was this church? He had heard alarming stories about heavy authority, shepherds who dictated to their flocks and ruled their lives. Was it true? Would they snatch his girl from him?

No, it wasn't true. He soon realised that Bob Cheeseman was a friend to her and it was natural for her to want to talk over the future direction of her life with him. Sometimes it happens naturally within families. I feel it certainly should happen, when necessary, within the life of both the nuclear Christian family and the wider family of the church.

We often had cause for amusement as different misunderstandings were related to us. Unfortunately, many people just accepted what they heard, failing to find out first hand whether the alleged facts were true or not.

'Arranged marriages are the thing at Bermondsey Christian Fellowship,' was a rumour circulating around a local hospital's Christian Union at one time. Bob and I heard about it when two of our single girls turned up to see us.

'Why haven't you arranged ours yet? Where are our husbands then?' they jokingly demanded.

Community of goods

We believed that our love for one another should be expressed practically and we were learning to do it.

'Learn to share your ordinary things, like lawnmowers,' one visiting preacher exhorted us. 'It saves expense and you bless each other.'

At that time only two families in the church had gardens so the illustration was unfortunate, but we understood the principle. Cars were loaned frequently and babysitters offered their services free. Meals were prepared for each other.

A fellowship fund was started up as a means of helping those in financial need. Help was given to enable some to have holidays.

Others needed debts covered, having got into difficulties

through unwise use of credit cards or failure to budget. We learned the best ways of dealing with these situations. If possible, we paid the debt or took it over so that no more interest was incurred. Sometimes we worked with the bank to get accounts in order. Then we gave guidance on how to budget and organise disciplined spending.

Paul and Barnabas

BCF was jokingly called the 'Bob and Chris Fellowship'. One couple nicknamed us Paul and Barnabas. It showed the extent of our mutual love, commitment and unity, as well as the difference in our characters.

'Do everything you can together at first,' John Houghton had counselled.

Practically, we worked well together. In helping others we had great times. 'I set them up, Bob hits them and then I pick them up again,' we joked together. Amazingly, people appreciated the input. It was a new situation for both Bob and me. We had both been on our own before; now we were a partnership with no clear leader. We fast became very interdependent.

'In working with Bob there is always the danger of competing with him. The Lord has rebuked me for this. There is absolutely no need to strive for position in his kingdom,' reads one of my diary notes for 1980.

Being human, we needed to resist any rival spirit. We were in this together to see God's plan fulfilled. We spent a lot of time talking and praying but not getting nearly as much done as we expected.

Elders in the gate

We believed from Scripture that it was the responsibility of elders to stand at the gate of the fold so that 'wild beasts' could not get in to hurt the flock.

Wild beasts? Some people might well mock. We would

disagree. One function of those delegated to lead God's people is to discern 'wolves' who may wish to enter for the wrong reasons. This is just one reason why we interview each person who wants to come into membership with us. If something goes very wrong, the person knows who is in charge.

Another reason is to ensure that Christians understand about the church, know what they are committing themselves to and what they can expect to receive. We wanted to make it clear that if we felt things were wrong in their lives, we would challenge them.

In the past we had been keen to see as many people as possible join us. Nothing wrong with that, of course, but coupled with it was an unhealthy fear of losing them. Winning people and keeping them had often meant a lack of honest confrontation when their lives hadn't been right.

'I only speak to my flock about spiritual things, not other matters,' one pastor told me. I couldn't agree to do the same because I had come to see that the Bible makes no distinction. True spirituality means doing *everything* for God, whether it be washing the kitchen floor or preaching on Sunday. God gives us spiritual life so that our whole bodies can be offered to him (Romans 12:1).

We found that our people were relieved that someone was going to cover them in all areas of their lives. They had often longed for such input.

'This is what I've been looking for,' many said to us.

As leaders, no longer were we afraid of confrontation. We were in charge because God had put us in charge. No longer would we be nice just for fear of upsetting people. Acting out of love sometimes meant being very firm. We also laid ourselves open to rebuke from others.

Surprised by joy

Each would-be member was asked to go through a foundational Bible study course. Through it they got a clear understanding of exactly what we believed. It included God's judgment, salvation through Christ, the work of God's Spirit, baptism in water and what 'church' really was.

After the course, we as elders interviewed each person. At first we always did it together. Later, as our numbers grew, this was not practical. I enjoyed these interviews. It is always great to hear first hand what God is doing in someone's life.

We asked a series of practical questions as well. What are you good at? What do you enjoy doing? Can you use these gifts in the fellowship?

The interviews didn't always go according to plan.

'Have you been baptised in the Spirit?' we asked a Chinese nurse.

'I'm not sure,' she replied. Clearly she lacked assurance.

'Would you like us to pray for you now?'

'Yes, please,' she answered shyly.

We prayed. It became impossible to continue the interview. God's Spirit fell upon her and she became radiant and bubbling with joy. We praised God together.

Each new member had to have been baptised in water before being accepted into BCF. We believed that the New Testament norm was repentance and faith followed very soon by baptism in water and baptism in the Holy Spirit. There were, of course, exceptions. A girl under eighteen, whose parents would not agree to it, was accepted into membership and she was baptised when she was old enough.

Two Lansdowne ladies had never been baptised. As one had severe arthritis and the other was elderly, Bob and I decided not to insist. Imagine our joy when both, quite separately, decided later that they wanted to be baptised.

More sensitive problems came with those who had been christened as babies and whose parents were genuine Christians. Having acted in sincerity for the children's good, the parents often protested at what they regarded as rebaptism.

'I want to be baptised but my parents feel it isn't necessary,' one student explained. It gave her a problem because she didn't want to upset them.

It wasn't easy for any of us. God had obviously honoured their faith for their child – after all, she was wanting to follow God. But that didn't make the ceremony in infancy a valid baptism. Baptism in the New Testament was clearly undergone because of a believer's own faith, not because of the faith of someone else.

In our church today parents give thanks to God for the birth of their newborn babies and publicly dedicate themselves to bringing them up in God's way. The church as a whole promises to stand by families in helping this to happen. Then, later, the child takes its own decision over baptism.

The sanctuary

So Bermondsey Christian Fellowship got under way. We were learning to submit ourselves in love to one another out of reverence for Christ. Christ was the Head of his body, the church, and as we learned to function together we brought honour to him.

We continued to use both buildings. Lansdowne was by far the older and, having been a mission hall, had never acquired pews. Everything about it was informal. Union Chapel, by contrast, was newer, with a very well-designed main hall or 'sanctuary'. Unlike Lansdowne it had been a 'proper' church and looked very nice with its light-oak pews, matching raised pulpit and pipe organ. It had a central aisle down its gently sloping floor and was really an auditorium, designed to seat folk listening to preaching.

It was inhibiting for more informal worship so we decided to remove the pulpit, pews and organ and level the floor. It seemed a great shame to spoil the careful design, but buildings are our servants, not our masters. While the work was being done we used a side hall, not so elegant but more suitable for our needs.

As time went on we faced difficulties over the character of

the two Sunday meetings. If one went well the other seemed to lack something.

We resolved this: the morning remained much the same, with worship and main teaching session, but we changed the evening. Here we concentrated on 'body ministry', seeking to draw people out more from themselves, and we broke bread together.

We were continuing to learn.

The Walworth group

A few months after the start of BCF we were interested to hear of a small group from Walworth who wanted to join with us. Several years later we talked to one of the members.

'We were really scared of coming in with you,' she recalled, 'but we knew it was right.'

She told us how, several years before, she had been attending a local church. 'I was very anti-charismatic when I first went there but I knew there was something missing in my Christian life. I was searching for a deeper relationship with God, and thought most other Christians were, too.

'I read the book, *Nine O'clock in the Morning,* and received the baptism in the Spirit on my own at home. I knew I had found what I'd been looking for. I was thrilled with God and my life had a new depth to it.'

Very soon afterwards she discovered a few others in the church who were also baptised in the Spirit. One of these was Sid Ancient.

A local lad, Sid had been dramatically saved at twenty years of age in a black church in Brixton and his life had changed completely. Soon afterwards he was baptised in God's Spirit. He was 'on fire', wanting everyone to know what he had found. He did lots of door-to-door visiting, taking the gospel to those who would listen, but somehow he didn't feel really at home in the local Baptist church. Although he and his wife, Doreen, attended, he didn't feel free to take people there. Not wanting to cause a problem, he sought out the pastor to talk to him about his feelings.

'Supernatural workings are for now, not just for New Testament times,' Sid reasoned.

'Well, you can be charismatic if you wish, but it would be best not to advertise it,' his pastor counselled.

Sid was asked to run a weeknight beginners' group. The group was lively and, because it was open, others joined in. The pastor would have liked to see the openness and sharing of experiences included in other church meetings. Sid thought it was unlikely to happen without an open acceptance of freedom in the Spirit.

Eventually the church leadership made a firm statement against the freer worship, feeling that it was not right. Sid and others of like mind graciously withdrew and met together as a housegroup. Though reluctant to begin with, Sid agreed to lead it.

At first, things went well. Others were converted and added to them. But as time went on Sid felt the strain. Being primarily an evangelist, he found himself unable to cope with the pastoral problems.

'We'd been getting some fellowship from a lively church in Streatham,' he recalls, 'and from some of the celebration meetings in Lewisham and Catford. We'd also been to a Downs Bible Week and one or two united meetings in Bermondsey.

'All of us were feeling the need to belong to something larger. There was no big word from God; it just seemed right to ask if we could join with BCF. I felt as if I was turning up with a lorry-load of materials and saying to Bob and Chris, "Please sign for the responsibility of these people."'

In response, Bob and I did some Bible studies with the housegroup. Then, after talking it over with John Houghton, we interviewed each individual and 'Sid's Group' became part of BCF in the autumn of 1980. They settled in quickly and we were delighted to have them.

Several told us afterwards how overwhelmingly grateful

they were to have found a live fellowship so close to home.

Finding our place

'I was still a bit scared of "restoration churches",' one Walworth lady remembers. 'BCF seemed so big, although only forty-five-strong, compared with our small group of ten.' She recalled how they all came together in a minibus – they were too afraid to come separately!

'One chap on the door was always so pleased to see us that he gave great big hugs. It was all a bit overpowering. We'd push each other forward saying, "You go first!" But we knew we'd have to overcome our nervousness and get involved.'

Sid himself remembers feeling a bit empty at first and needed time to 'find himself' again. His people still turned to him with their problems and it all took a little time to take on a new pattern. He wanted to level out and pick up what God wanted him to do, even if that did mean being asked to run a homegroup! He was longing to get involved in door-to-door work again.

Readjusting

It wasn't only the Walworth members who found they needed time to settle down. Feelings of vulnerability were fairly common among other members after the 'marriage'. Each person had to readjust.

Previously, church life had been centred around activities and meetings. We now had a policy of keeping organised activities to a minimum. Even the attempts we made at special evangelism fell flat. There seemed to be no life in them.

The Lord reminded us again that we should do 'no uncommanded work'. For a time he was clearly directing us to give priority to the church. It troubled us a little for we knew that God had commanded the church to preach the gospel and we were there to reach the community.

It troubled some people, too, because their security had been in what they did rather than in God himself. With some of those activities gone there were pastoral problems to deal with. These were heightened by our Spirit-filled worship. It was difficult to keep some problems hidden when there was such an atmosphere of warmth and love.

'A sign spoken against'

We were thrilled to find that one or two pastors in our immediate area were in sympathy with us. A local Baptist man was seeking to lead his people in a similar direction to us. We had good fellowship. Another leader also reacted positively.

'God's blessing on you will lead to the blessing of all of us,' he remarked.

Sadly, there were lots of negative reactions from some Christians. They were suspicious of our change of direction and, although we had experienced good fellowship in the past, it became difficult to maintain.

We enjoyed some evenings which we named 'All Saints Nights'. Christians came to them from many different churches with great enthusiasm. But these meetings lost impetus. Their purpose had never been well-defined and, as far as fellowship with other Christians was concerned, it became clear that 'for two to walk together they must be agreed'.

These negative developments obviously caused us distress. We couldn't help being what we were, but to express it caused offence. We wanted unity with others but our attempts were not meeting with success. Perhaps we wanted too much too soon.

I remember being at a united prayer meeting where unity was the main theme. I had one of my first pictures or visions from God. It was very vivid.

At first I couldn't make it out. Then I realised it was an image of a mountain gully in which flowed a stream. As the stream continued on its way down the gully it was joined later by another gully with its stream, then still later others came in so that eventually a great river flowed out.

I felt the Lord saying that we should follow the direction he was giving to us and let him bring us together with others in his own time and way. To attempt to get through the rock to another gully would be fruitless.

Christ's prayer is 'that all of them may be one, even as we are one'. Others who live by God's Word may be in a different gully from us but we will all end up together. I pray for every stream to be blessed so that it happens sooner rather than later.

Sadly, some so-called Christian churches are preaching another gospel. We don't believe in identifying ourselves with another gospel. We do believe that eventually God will bring his *true* church to unity, to present a glorious, spotless bride to Christ.

Housegroups

Towards the end of 1980, John Houghton talked to us about housegroups. As the church grew, it would become easier to care for people in smaller groups. It would also help them to find themselves and learn to relate to others. What's more, giving younger potential leaders responsibility for the groups would help them to grow into leadership.

We also needed to prepare the church for further growth, John said. Healthy churches can expect to produce babies.

So Bob and I set about selecting leaders. We chose three couples whom we felt were best fitted for the task. John then gave them some help in understanding what housegroups were meant to be.

They were to be cells within the church of people who belonged together, each caring for the others in whatever way might be necessary. They were not just a replacement for the midweek meeting; they were to give opportunity for sharing meals, possessions, needs and experiences, as well as singing 'psalms and hymns and spiritual songs' and following up the Sunday teaching.

We had to decide who was to go into which group. It was no good having a number of elderly people in one group and no-one with a car for transporting them; neither did we want all the musicians in the same group.

Early days

London flats don't usually have large living-rooms. House-group meetings could be a bit like playing 'sardines'. David and Lesley Nunn, who led one of these first housegroups, remember it well.

'As it grew we had as many as thirty people. Even when twenty turned up we were packed really tightly into our small front room. Because it was long and narrow, when we stood up to sing we could almost rub noses!'

On another occasion Dave wanted to divide his people up into three groups to pray. One group stayed in the sitting-room, another went into the small kitchen and another went on to the landing at the top of the stairs. This last group, for lack of space, opened the bathroom door and invited the elderly member to sit on the loo. The others crowded round, sitting or standing, and got down to prayer.

We would have had smaller housegroups sooner but we were always short of leaders.

So folk settled in, learning to share their lives and overcome inhibitions. Not everyone found it easy. It was a learning situation and some preconceived ideas had to be *un*learned. Some people, for example, had been brought up not to go into others' homes for a meal. A cup of tea, yes, but offering or accepting a meal wasn't done.

At the opposite end of the scale, others had to grasp the truth of Proverbs 25:17, learning to respect privacy and not always be in their Christian neighbours' homes.

Hardly polished, a bit naive perhaps, but it was a joy and a thrill to be part of BCF in those early days.

8

Still in the battle

'Why did your heads go down this morning?' David Nunn asked those present at a Sunday evening meeting in May 1981.

At first I was surprised by his question but quickly realised that he was helping people to be honest following the morning message.

I had preached from Acts 4:31. We could speak the word of God boldly because we knew the Sovereign Lord and because we were filled with his Spirit. We could hold our heads high and be bold before the world outside – in theory. But in practice we often didn't do it. We felt ourselves to be a small, insignificant, embattled minority. The oppressiveness of the city, the dirt, the crowds, the noise and traffic, the graffiti, the cold apathy of the people were constant pressures which sapped our time and energy.

Just surviving seemed to take all our strength. It was hard to think of ourselves reaching out to the community 'boldly'.

General unrest

There was also a lot of general unrest in inner cities around that time.

'I remember 1981 for the Brixton riots,' one of our sons remarked to us when we were talking about the early days of BCF. He was thirteen at the time and remembers the general unrest in our area, too.

Rivalry between two nearby schools resulted in 'war' between them, as gangs of children mounted attacks and counter-attacks on each other after school. Shopkeepers went to the lengths of boarding up their shops on the strength of one rumour of impending trouble.

Gangs of bored youths roamed the streets looking for excitement in their dull lives. Some were playing truant from school, others couldn't get jobs, still others wouldn't even look for employment.

Sue remembers talking to a local lady in her forties who was shaking with fear as she passed on news that gangs of youths had attacked a shopping centre a few miles away.

'I'm going straight home and will lock myself in,' she confided.

It was no wonder our church was to us like an oasis in the desert.

'I only stay in this area because of the church,' expressed one young person. The same was true for many within the family of inner-city Christians.

The following few years proved to be a time of learning to break through our difficulties. We prayed together, stood in support of one another as various problems arose, helped in every way possible and found encouragement from the Bible. Love flowed between us.

Housing

One of our biggest needs was for accommodation. At the time only two and a half per cent of the population in our district owned their own homes, eighty per cent rented council property, mostly flats, and the remainder rented from private landlords or housing associations. The council operated a points system and the waiting-lists were very long. To buy a home was almost impossible.

As we prayed, one after another were supplied with flats – legally! It would have been easier had they been prepared to be dishonest. 'Just tell them you're a nurse,' one trainee dentist was advised.

'I could offer you a flat if you were pregnant,' single girls were told.

We prayed couples into flats after housing officials had said they didn't stand a chance because they hadn't been on the waiting-list long enough. Some were 'hard to let' flats, which meant that they were often not so nice, or the block had a bad reputation. Some members took quite grotty accommodation in order to stay.

'If God wants people to join us, he'll provide them with flats,' we thought. So we prayed again and again.

Jobs

As time went on, the unemployment rate in the country rose. We prayed for jobs for our members and mostly saw them provided. Using the fellowship fund, we enabled some to set up in self-employment. This was no huge scheme but we provided ladders for window cleaners, a van for a decorator or help with a smashed car used for work.

Some Christian organisations went further, setting up workshops where men and women could learn new trades. We were not able to go that far but we did believe God equipped us, his church, to help meet the needs of our own people.

Racial harassment

Most of us found it a trial living in the inner city, but for some the experience was sometimes almost unbearable. The following story illustrates this.

It concerns a young couple and their three children. Mum was black; Dad was white. Often, when the children went out to play, they would be picked on and called 'Paki' and other names. It was never easy for them.

One day we were returning with them from a church-run holiday. I had left Sue and the children in the minibus while I helped the family up the stairs with their luggage. When we got to the door of their flat, it was open – entry had been forced. As if that wasn't enough, no-one had reported it to the caretaker or to the police. People had just walked in and out, helping themselves to what they wanted. Even the kitchen table and chairs and the nicer house plants had gone.

This wasn't the last break-in they experienced and the racial harassment continued. Often we gathered round them and prayed for strength and peace to be given. We also prayed for rehousing and wrote to the local Member of Parliament. Eventually they were moved to where the pressures weren't so great.

This was a fairly extreme though not an isolated case. We helped each other not only to cope in such situations but to experience God's righteousness, peace and joy in the Holy Spirit, so triumphing in him.

We talked through the practical issues. How do you cope when your children are picked on? Do you confront those who are doing wrong or do you just pray? How can you love your neighbours when their dog fouls your stairway or they keep you awake with their parties or arguments? What were God's answers to these and other problems?

Bringing up children

Often with no mothers or grandmothers around, and no garden in which children could play, young mums felt isolated and under pressure. Some tried local playgroups but found not all of them were of a good standard.

One young mother in our church set up a mums and toddlers group. She also asked permission to take over a small area round the back of Union Chapel. Here she had a sand-pit laid out and a turfed area where the children could play. They planted some flowers and enjoyed their 'garden' and the opportunity to sit, chat and encourage one another.

Older women were free to pop in if they wished and lend a listening ear or give words of encouragement, as well as to enjoy the children.

'We've done it all before'

As we learned to overcome our various problems, our confidence grew.

God's purpose for his church is that all peoples on earth will be blessed through us. A sanctuary, a safe place, a family, yes – but also an army unit, a battle outpost. He had given us weapons to use, including having our feet fitted with the gospel of peace (Ephesians 6:15).

Our heads had gone down in response to the exhortation to be bold, not only because of the struggles I have just mentioned, but also because we felt that, when it came to planned evangelism, we had done it all before. Many times in past years we had preached the gospel and done door-to-door visiting, but with very little fruit. At Lansdowne for years we had pushed literature through thousands of letterboxes and given out invitations to services at Christmas, Easter and Harvest. We were weary of it. Was it worth trying again?

'Lord, I need a fresh heart for the gospel,' I wrote in my diary at that time.

I, in particular, felt in need of stirring. My gift was primarily that of a pastor and I was happy and fulfilled caring for the people of God. When I needed to have a short stay in hospital in 1981, church members came to visit me. Before long, they would raise issues which concerned them. We talked them over and they went away helped.

'What an attractive ministry, lying in bed helping people!' I thought. But I knew I mustn't stop there. My pastoral gift didn't let me off the hook over evangelism.

Spreading the gospel

Although Bob and I had encouraged the church to evangelise, we hadn't made much headway. But that was about to change.

Terry Virgo had encouraged us to invite Ben Davies, from

Bracknell, to talk to the church on evangelism. Until that time we had invited evangelists to do our gospel preaching for us. But Ben came, talked to the church, and overnight our people were motivated, excited and full of faith to see others saved through them.

It opened our eyes to understand 'the work of an evangelist' in the way 2 Timothy 4 and Ephesians 4 speak of that gift. Ben really did 'equip the saints', building us up and helping us to see God's kingdom grow.

The place buzzed. We began to see more guests join us.

Learning to pray

We prayed expectantly, in a way previously unknown.

'Pray for your neighbours,' was a key theme for us. Folk set prayer goals for the people around them. We learned to wait on God and hear what he had to say, so that we could pray in faith.

'I've just got a picture from God,' shared one lady when we were all praying about getting to know our neighbours. 'I don't understand it – it's a fruit-cake!'

While some puzzled over the meaning, to others it was quite clear: she should bake a cake for her neighbour. Sure enough, it proved to be the opening in that home, breaking the former unfriendliness.

'I've lived in my flat for twelve years,' someone else shared, 'but until yesterday I'd never had any conversation with my neighbours. We met when I was putting my milk bottles out, then chatted over a cup of tea.'

Our prayers were again breaking down barriers, creating neighbourliness instead of the isolation caused by selfishness, fear or prejudice. So the stories went on, helping to increase our faith and spurring us on to pray.

As well as the normal prayer meetings we had days of prayer, prayer partnerships of three or four people and early morning prayer. In these times we reached out to God, asking him to have mercy and save people.

Deliverance and healing

God continued to equip us and teach us new lessons. As his Spirit was demonstrated among us we learned more also about the power of the enemy. Evil spirits are still alive and active and responsible for more than we give them credit for.

Our eyes were opened as we listened to men and women ministering in the supernatural, discerning spirits and rebuking them in Jesus' name. We read books on deliverance and healing and later on learned a great deal from the John Wimber conferences. All we gleaned we then adapted and used in our own situations.

For a time we were inclined to see demonic activity in almost any problem we encountered, but with experience we grew in discernment. We learned to confront the enemy spirits responsible for some fears, illnesses and bad habits and in the name of Jesus cast them out.

One Sunday, after a baptism, I was called to counsel a powerfully-built man sitting in the front row. I squatted in front of him and talked to him of the grace of God. At first his head was bowed but suddenly he roared, sprang forwards and pushed me backwards towards the baptistry. I was glad to know the power of the name of Jesus as I roared back, rebuking the demon. As I did so the man moved back calmly into his seat.

'Pray for the sick'

In the area of physical healing we were learning as well. From time to time we came across men with healing ministries. A few left us with more questions than they answered but on the whole our faith was stirred. We learned to pray more positively and to use words of knowledge from God.

Calling for the elders to pray over sick people and anoint them with oil (see James 5:14-15) became a more common practice. We were recognising that healing the sick was linked with our great commission to preach the gospel.

As we prayed for people in our Sunday services we saw physical reactions to God's power. Some people visibly shook or openly wept. It was something of a shock when people first started to fall over when being prayed for. It was alarming for those who had never seen it before, especially if it was a loved one stretched out on the floor. It was great to see changes in all of us as we responded to each others' prayers.

One baby girl was losing weight rapidly through persistent vomiting. The whole church prayed one Sunday evening.

'I had a vision as we were praying,' one young nurse told us. 'The sun was going down but, just as it seemed to be setting, it came up again.'

We continued to pray. Over the next couple of weeks the hospital did many tests but they were inconclusive. The baby just got weaker until, one weekend, the parents realised she was about to die.

'I gave her up to the Lord,' the mother said. 'I could see the end was near.'

Then God stepped in. The 'sun rose again' and the little girl started putting on weight, becoming strong and healthy.

So we began to see God's power demonstrated in a new way. It was still something of a mystery, for God is sovereign, but now we were expecting more from him in these areas.

Battle cell

I will close this chapter by telling you about one of our house-groups – later called homegroups because a lot were 'flat'-groups!

The couple who ran this group had a clear vision for what they wanted to do. They saw themselves as a battle unit within the church. They prayed for their block of flats (their flat was one of those provided by God in answer to our prayers), put on films in the local tenants' hall, joined the local tenants' association and did door-to-door visiting with the gospel.

They met each week to worship and praise God and give each other support. So they were strengthened for their task.

The run-down block had a bad reputation and there were many tensions among the residents. Later, the couple were delighted to have some other Christians come to live in the same block, but it was still far from easy for any of them. They endured having eggs thrown at them, break-ins, windows being broken or knocked on late at night in order to disturb them. Most of the aggro stemmed from a group of men, one in particular, out of work, who just hated Christians.

The couple knew they had the answer for these people and set out to be friendly in answer to the abuse hurled at them. The wife was at home much of the time looking after her small children. She saw other people as she hauled children and pushchair up and down the stairs and hung washing out on the balcony outside the flat door.

Many people would not have endured what those Christians endured. Without the same strength of local church backing, others with a similar vision have fallen by the wayside. As it was, they continued to fight in this dark place and at times grew very weary.

There was the time when their toddler dropped a toy car through the balcony railings on to the bonnet of a car in the square three floors below. Obviously a bad dent was made. And who should the car belong to but the ringleader of the opposition group! A lot of unpleasantness followed, even though our friends paid for the damage.

Another time the wife talked to Sue: 'I just feel worn out with my neighbour. She's always knocking on the door to borrow things or to use the phone. Her children come in and do just what they want. She never corrects them, even if they break toys or other things. I've tried to be friendly but find myself resenting her.'

After talking things over, she went back to take command of the situation. She realised her actions should be under God's direction, not dictated by the neighbour, no matter how needy the lady was.

'I told her she could use the phone only for an emergency,

that she could come in for coffee only when I invited her and that she must control her children,' she shared later. 'Learning to say "no" set me free, and I realised it was part of the expression of my love for the woman.'

The couple together continued to try showing the woman and her husband that Jesus could help them. There was little fruit at the time but the seed had been sown.

The oppressiveness in the block began to ease. The Christians prayed about the problem of the men causing trouble. The unexpected answer came by way of many of them getting jobs. This broke up the gang, making it better for everyone.

They also prayed that the forces of darkness would be overcome. A local vicar walked through the block one day. 'The atmosphere has changed,' he told us. 'I was pleasantly surprised. The block is still run-down but it's different.'

The Member of Parliament for our constituency of Southwark, Simon Hughes, is a Christian. He has worked hard for local people and all recognise his genuine concern. He spoke one day to a small group of us.

'With prayer support, I can work in Parliament to change our land, but what I can do is so small,' he said. 'You people do the real work as you introduce Jesus to your neighbours. Then, as he changes households up and down the country, so our nation will be changed.'

Does it excite you? Each Christian with terrific potential to change history. As we are willing to move under God, live where he wants us to live, use his weapons to bring light into the darkness, we – the church – will win.

9

Schools and schooling

'I don't want to go to school!' our fearful five-year-old cried.

He endorsed his feelings by refusing to put on his shoes and get ready. The inevitable battle of wills followed, ending up with Sue and our two youngest boys trudging along to school five minutes late, far from serene. This upsetting episode was becoming more frequent. Sue was used to riding similar storms but this seemed different. Our concern was growing.

Sue talked to other mums in the playground and found that they were also having problems.

'He used to like school,' one mum said, 'but since he's been in this new class he just doesn't want to go.'

'Not only is he unhappy but he doesn't seem to be learning anything,' commented another mum worriedly.

Sue and I paid the headteacher several visits. She was helpful and appeared to take our concerns seriously. Eventually some of the rowdy boys in the class, who had been bent on bullying the younger ones, were split up. Things improved slightly, but we suspected that our five-year-old was just being allowed to play all day.

'I can't help it if he wants to play in the sandtray and not read,' was his teacher's defensive reply to our probing questions.

This easy-going approach was proving disastrous for our boy. The philosophy seemed to be: 'Children will learn in the end; we mustn't force them.'

We were disappointed. We had so wanted to be fully part of the local community but now we were in a dilemma. Our eight-year-old was thriving under a different teacher in the same school but, overall, the school's reputation had worsened. Many mums were complaining that their children were not learning. What should we do?

High ideals

Christian leaders in areas like ours reacted in different ways to the education problem. Some would move to a better area when their children came up to school age. Some would send their children to schools further out from the inner city, sometimes paying for their education. Others would find themselves within the catchment area of a good school and remain reasonably happy with the education provided there.

When Sue and I had first moved into Bermondsey we had fixed ideals. We were aware that generally the standards in inner-city schools were not as good as those in suburban areas, but we felt we could trust God for our children. We believed home to be the greatest influence on them, and their going to local schools enabled us all to be fully part of the community. If our children had academic ability and lost out earlier on, they would catch up later.

Over the years our ideals caused us a lot of heart-searching. We found it much easier to trust God for finance than for our children's welfare. From time to time we seriously thought of moving away from the inner city for their sakes.

The pressure increases

From around 1981 to 1983 these family pressures heightened in intensity. I have related what was happening to our youngest, but he wasn't the only one suffering. Our older children sometimes felt socially isolated. Their upbringing marked them out from their peers. They didn't feel at home in an increasingly materialistic and violent society.

'Why do you act so posh yet you've got nothing?' was a scathing question asked of one of our boys at secondary school. It showed the value which many put on 'things' and the prejudices against those who were 'different'.

'Why have you brought me up to be different from the rest?' he railed on us at one time, expressing the pressure he was under. The acute pain and rejection he felt eventually caused him to rebel against us and God. It was a very hard time for us all.

Another of our boys didn't feel the social stigma as acutely but was still suffering at school from lack of help, especially with his English. This affected his education later.

A Christian school

While we were under these pressures the subject of Christian education arose from more than one source. Until that time, sending our children to a Christian school wasn't an option we had considered. Now it seemed to be shouting at us.

We discovered that the then Mile End Christian Fellowship, just opposite us on the north side of the Thames, had recently started their own school. The pupils were from Christian families within their fellowship, plus a few others.

In 1983 we moved house and so had to find a new school for our children. A friend, now a full-time pastor but formerly a school-teacher, pointed out the weakness in one of the main arguments against taking children out of state education: the Scripture verse, 'You are the salt of the earth' (Matthew 5:13).

Many Christians thought that acting as salt and light in society included keeping our children in local schools. But my friend pointed out that, in Bible times, salt was used as a disinfectant, and it was not sprinkled on but applied by the shovelful! He felt the burden was too much for our children – only one or two Christians in schools of over a thousand.

Mission workers in pagan countries overseas had long ago recognised the need for Christian schools. Now Britain, once known as a Christian country, had become largely pagan as well. I wouldn't send my children to an Islamic school, so why send them to a humanist school?

I saw the problems clearly now. Most subjects were taught with a humanist bent which detracted from God and elevated man. I could also see that peer pressure on my children was proving too much for them. And, not least, they were just not getting a good standard of education.

Step of faith

So it was that, in September 1983, we decided to send three of our children to Shekinah Christian School in Tower Hamlets.

It was a step of faith. Even though the fees were modest, we didn't really have enough income to pay them, having just taken out a mortgage. Also, the school was small – what if it folded? Our children would find it even more difficult then to go back into state education.

As it seemed such a big step to take, Sue and I decided not to encourage other parents in the same direction until we had tried it out ourselves first. Shortly after hearing about it, however, four other parents had also decided to send their children. There was no holding them, in spite of my counsel to take time to weigh up the pros and cons. They saw the opportunity as the Lord's answer for their offspring. Like us, for a long time they had felt themselves to be fighting a losing battle.

After a very short time the positive comments were many.

'He's much happier and more settled.'

'She's taking a pride in her work now.'

'He's being praised for each effort he makes. It helps him get over his frustration at being slow.'

'They look forward to going to school now, they enjoy it so much.'

The opening question to us as we sat down for a parent-teacher chat was, 'Have you had any words from God for him?'

School reports gave assessments on each child's emotional and spiritual state, on his or her attitude towards staff and on academic ability. The pupils were encouraged to forgive when wronged and taught how to pray in every aspect of their lives.

Shekinah Christian School

The school had been started as a venture by the Mile End Christian Fellowship. The use of an American educational system enabled it to get off the ground without trained teachers. The Lord provided a building – an old church-school institute – which was gradually refurbished, helped by grants. Parents were asked to pay fees, but no child was barred admission because they couldn't afford it. The church heavily subsidised the running costs and salaries.

Part of the original vision was to teach each pupil a practical skill, so enabling them to earn their living by it. This has not yet been realised.

The staff worked for a pittance at first. Any mothers or fathers with special skills contributed according to what time they had available. It was sheer hard work. The odds were against the school's success. The church was far from wealthy, there was no pool of teachers to draw upon and the facilities for secondary education were very limited.

Her Majesty's Inspector's report

Our own church gradually became more involved. Union Chapel in Tooley Street was used to house the lower age group when increased numbers necessitated the formation of more classes. We ran a financial support scheme within the church to help parents to pay fees. The struggle to find enough staff and finance continued.

Then came the first visit of Her Majesty's Inspector of Schools. Their report was devastating. Not only did they criticise the narrowness of the American system but pointed out the need for qualified staff and better equipment. The school would not receive registration until we acted on their recommendations. Even then it would not automatically follow.

On the positive side, they picked out the happiness of the children and the very good relationship between them and the staff. That was in spite of our using corporal punishment for some offenders – something which is now banned in most British schools!

Unfortunately, all the thirteen- and fourteen-year-olds had to leave and go back into state schools. The secondary curriculum just wasn't developed enough to be able to keep them. The transition worked well for some but not for others. We were sorry to see them go.

We sweated and prayed. Obviously we needed some trained teachers who could help broaden the curriculum. And we desperately needed more finance, not only for equipment but also to pay the staff more realistic salaries. How could we ask teachers to come from the state system and take huge pay drops? Certainly a married person with a family to support could not have managed on what we were paying.

God answered our prayers. The inspectors came back, before the next official visit was due, to advise on our progress. Shortly afterwards, in 1986, we received full registration. They didn't need another visit. Great was our jubilation! God had proved faithful yet again.

Is it all worth it?

That certainly wasn't the end of all our troubles. Shortage of staff and finance still continue to plague the school, although sometimes there have been dramatic answers to prayer.

At the time of writing, we have sadly learned that the school is not able to continue at secondary level. The demands of providing a full examination syllabus have proved too much. The junior section of the school, however, is progressing well.

'Is it all worth it?' some might ask. The answer for me is

very definitely, 'Yes – especially in the inner city.'

The reason for my certainty is threefold. First, we saw the effect on our own children. They changed dramatically. Their tensions eased as they responded to the loving, disciplined atmosphere. They no longer had to put up with a double standard between home and school. They learned to set themselves goals within their achievement ability and were encouraged for every effort.

We noticed that they were able to mix better with children in the local park. When we had taken our children out of the local school we feared in case they would then feel more inhibited with others. Instead, the opposite was true: their security produced more self-confidence. It was good to see it. They didn't have masses of equipment or large playgrounds but they did have everything centred on God and his standard.

My second reason for believing it to be worthwhile is the benefit to families who want to stay to strengthen the church in the inner city but are put off by the general standard of many schools. This was the price Sue and I had had to pay for serving God in the inner city and the one which caused us the most heart-searching. Knowing that children are safe and properly cared for eases the situation considerably.

And, third, the Christian school is excellent for the children of parents who have recently come to God. Fresh out of the world, these new Christians themselves need so much teaching on kingdom principles. If the church helps them by providing Christian education for their children, the whole family can more quickly grow into maturity under God's authority.

No hard-and-fast rules

All parents under God have to decide what they believe is best for their children. This will inevitably vary from area to area and from child to child. Some are fortunate enough to be in the catchment area of good schools. Even then, much vigilance is needed.

Other parents, seeing a lack within their local state schools, will be inventive and energetic enough to supply their children with supplementary programmes of activities. But not all parents are gifted in that way.

We are convinced that all things work together for the good of those who love God. Sue and I found ourselves in situations with the children which hurt. God didn't let us down, even though it may have appeared that way at times. We are pleased to tell you that our rebel is now the best of friends both with us and with God!

Sometimes I have been asked by people from outside how they can help in the school. Prayer, staff and finance are the main needs.

The heading for this chapter could have been the same as chapter eight – 'Still in the battle'. Anyone involved closely with Shekinah – soon to be renamed 'The Highway School' – will affirm this. A report on the school today could read: 'Has made considerable progress and shows promise for the future.'

10

Vineyard

'I've just had a picture from God,' a young Christian, quite new to our church, was sharing. 'I don't know what it means but it's very vivid.'

She described how she saw two pyramids of light, each with many facets which reflected the light at angles. They moved towards each other and then away again. Finally, they moved together and fused to become a sphere, giving uniform light all around.

We were amazed. This young woman couldn't possibly understand the implications of the picture. We were enjoying a united meeting with the Drummond Road Christian Fellowship. Our two churches had moved towards each other in the past but just recently had moved apart again. The message seemed very clear: we should join and become one body.

During the following months the word was tested and weighed. Bob and I shared it with John Houghton and Terry Virgo. We talked and prayed together, asking God to confirm it and asking how it could be worked out.

Drummond Road

Let me put you in the picture about Drummond Road Christian Fellowship.

They were a small group of people meeting in Drummond Road Baptist Church in Bermondsey. Charles Spurgeon had worked hard in London, not only in his own Metropolitan Tabernacle but also in founding missions and chapels which helped meet the desperate spiritual needs of the metropolis. The Baptist church in Drummond Road, capable of seating six hundred and fifty, was one of them. It was purchased in 1866 for £1500!

Twenty people from 'the Tabernacle' had been transferred to the new church, joining with nine newly-baptised members. Numbers had continued to grow and by 1882 there were four hundred and twenty-six.

As with all inner-city works, the history is chequered. One of the older members was converted there in the 1930s when she was sixteen.

'It was a lively fellowship with a growing membership,' she remembers. 'Every week folk were converted and baptisms came every month. Our pastor was a Spirit-filled Christian. We spoke in tongues and knew God was with us. Four or five missionaries went out from our fellowship to serve God overseas. Then came the war which broke things up. Many people were evacuated.'

Preparing for something new

In the 1970s, the Drummond Road group, though much smaller than formerly, still seemed to be thriving compared with other local churches. There was a large Sunday school and Girls' and Boys' Brigades.

One member there told me, 'In 1980 God began speaking to us about our organisations and the wrong place they had in our priorities. We were also receiving clear Bible teaching from our pastor and having to face up to some issues which previously we had played down. In particular, we had to come to terms with the person and work of the Holy Spirit, and his gifts for us in the church today.

'God spoke clearly to the leaders of the organisations, some quite independently of the others, to the effect that, for him to be glorified, the Brigades and the women's rally must close. There were a hundred and six in the Girl's Brigade alone, so it seemed a strange thing to do. But we understood that God was going to do a new work. The old structures must be completely razed in preparation.'

She remembers that they were difficult but exciting times. There was the first taste of a celebration meeting with other local churches, and the first Downs Bible Week. Sadly, some members didn't feel it was right and found other churches to attend. John Houghton continued to have input and they drew closer to BCF.

In the autumn of 1984, the fellowship at Drummond, now only twenty-one people plus children, found themselves without a leader. Bob and I agreed to help them until the end of the year. In the new year the people could decide whether or not they would join with BCF.

Although God had given clear direction, the people needed help in moving into it. We saw that it was important for the church to have a prophetic input and that it should be coupled with pastoral care. One factor without the other would cause problems.

It wasn't easy for them. Their loyalties to Drummond went deep. There were many questions about the building and the witness in the immediate locality. Some were sure about the move, while others had mixed feelings.

In January 1985 they finally decided to become part of BCF and we started meeting all together. They brought a new strength to us. Many had been Christians for some time and they had been well taught from the Scriptures.

'In looking back, many of the details have become faded with the passing of time,' wrote one Christian who had been converted in Drummond. 'The one thing remaining is that God's purposes have been and are being fulfilled in our area. God is building his church and the gates of hell shall not prevail against it.

'In it all, God has been so gracious, kind and patient with us, leading us from one step to the next with a Father's love and compassion.'

Another building

In addition to the Lansdowne and Union buildings, we now

had an even bigger one. We hadn't really been able to afford the first two, so how were we going to manage another?

Like Lansdowne, Drummond was old and in need of repair. The main church hall hadn't been used for some time. Yet what an opportunity! If we let it go we would be unlikely to find another place in our area seating so many people. When the church grew, we would be needing all the buildings we could get. It was another indication of God's future blessing.

We negotiated with the London Baptist Property Board, reassuring them that we could meet the requirements of the trust deed.

A new name

While all that was going on, so was the hunt for a new name. We no longer covered Bermondsey alone. We had people from Walworth, Camberwell and Rotherhithe and we wanted to show we recognised that the Drummond people were joining as equals. The two pyramids of light were joining to make one sphere.

We went through similar agonies to those of parents who can't at first decide on the right name for their child. Vineyard Community Church was one of the options.

I was reluctant. We were certain to be confused with John Wimber's Vineyard Fellowship from the USA. Then I was praying one day when God reminded me of his promise all those years before. 'Sow . . . reap . . . plant *vineyards.*' The other leaders were amused when I finally agreed – they had seen no problem with the name in the first place.

So September 1986 saw our name changed to Vineyard Community Church.

Anyone want to follow Jesus?

We began to see a steady trickle of converts. Many were local people with no church background. For years we had longed to see such people turn to Christ. The power of God was very evident in these conversions, producing dramatic change.

'If anyone would like to follow Jesus would they please come forward.'

A visiting speaker was concluding his message. The words were barely out of his mouth when a young lady sitting directly in front of him jumped up, completely obscuring his view.

'That's the quickest response I've ever had,' he commented as he peered around her to see others coming.

After one service a young lad came over and introduced himself to Sue and me. Slowly, recognition dawned on us. We had known him when he was at junior school. We had taken him to one Downs Bible Week where God had given him a vision of Jesus. His home situation had been desperate, with a violent alcoholic stepfather and a mother who couldn't cope. He had been taken into care away from London and we had lost contact.

Now he was standing in front of us wanting to come back to God. His heavenly Father had steered his path to cross with that of a Christian from our church who was working on a Salvation Army project for young homeless people. We were overjoyed when he was baptised soon afterwards.

'It's all right for you being a Christian – you've got a good education and speak nice. But it's not really for people like me,' said a Bermondsey dental nurse to a dentist who happened to be from our church. Some time later she came to a special service where a down-to-earth local man was preaching the gospel. He seemed to be talking directly to her. She found that God was as interested in her as he was in the dentist.

There followed a whole spate of miraculous conversions, some of which I related in the first chapter.

Worship – a powerful tool

We were seeing this tremendous impact on people through

our normal worship services. Some folk with church backgrounds were startled when they visited our services. The freedom and spontaneity, the use of the Spirit's gifts, our style of music and the noise level often hit them forcibly, if not always favourably!

Some non-Christians thought we were mad. Others were moved and shaken by the life, warmth and love. What they saw had a profound effect on them, even if they remembered very little of what they had heard.

Most working people are not swayed by closely reasoned arguments. Their opinions are formed by impressions and events. They understand 'concrete' rather than 'conceptual' language. Many had had an image of the church as a formal and insipid institution. As we worshipped in the Spirit they found themselves forced into the reality of God's presence. It had a powerful effect.

I remember, years before, taking some young men to hear a well-known evangelist. I was impressed with his reasoning and his oratory, but all my friends said was, 'Blimey, what a mouth!'

Bert Barritt, when speaking to the deaf, uses pictures as much as possible. It is far easier for them to have something to visualise than merely to have words. Most of us are the same. Jesus knew this, which is why he often spoke in parables and used everyday objects and events to illustrate what he had to say.

New Testament-type problems

We found ourselves dealing with what I call New Testament-type problems. When Paul wrote in his letters about paying taxes and debts, about sexual morality, drunkenness, greed, coarse joking, rage, anger, malice, gossiping and people who were work-shy, he was addressing situations that actually existed within the church. We were finding similar problems.

When a middle class man with a church background backslides from God, he usually manages to keep up an appearance of respectability. He may even continue to attend meetings although his heart is cold towards God. But when a new Christian, previously immoral, drunken or thieving, backslides, he tends to go back to his life of obvious sin. It may be a temporary lapse but the effects are far-reaching. It makes for a lot of pastoral work.

We often had a dilemma. We didn't want to be condemning, but neither could we countenance sin or let the church be identified with it. We wanted to be ready to forgive where there was genuine repentance. Sometimes repentance was easy to recognise; at other times it wasn't.

Sometimes freedom from drunkenness, violence, adultery or swearing came in a dramatic clean-up at conversion. In other cases fierce battles ensued, requiring specific prayer for deliverance. The enemy would be rebuked in the authority of the name of Jesus. The people concerned still needed prayer and pastoral care, but they were then able to make better progress.

'Now I knew I had a fair fight on my hands and that I had the power to win,' is how one man described his feelings after prayer for deliverance.

Giving up smoking was difficult for many. It wasn't unusual to see a small group of Christians standing outside just before meeting-time having a last drag, hoping they would then be able to last out until the end of the service. We wanted to help them kick the habit without looking down on them.

Repeatedly we prayed for wisdom and spent time talking about these and other problems.

Equipping and discipling new converts

'I just can't manage on one lot of Social Security money,' wailed one housewife. Since she and her common-law husband had become Christians they had stopped the lying which had enabled them to obtain a Social Security book each. Now they were in problems because they didn't know how to cope.

Others had persistently lived beyond their means, incurring debts which could take a lifetime to pay off.

Bob developed quite a ministry of helping these people with their finances. Telling them what to do was not enough. Counselling needed follow-up and discipleship. Wives who had learnt how to budget could pass on advice – how to think ahead and shop wisely, how to make cheaper meals and how to mend and make do.

Keeping a home clean, bringing up children, successful relationships – all needed direct teaching from the Scriptures and an example from others. Thus people were brought into maturity and in their turn could help others.

Many of these new converts were spiritually very aware. The power of God's Holy Spirit had come into their lives, contrasting starkly with the powers of darkness. Their eyes were opened and their experience of God was very real and obvious. Many received visions and a deep awareness of the supernatural.

They posed very different problems from those I was used to with my evangelical upbringing. I was accustomed to folk coming to the Lord through a clear teaching of the gospel. Such converts became very Word-centred, but most had little experience of God's Spirit.

By contrast, many of the new Christians for whom we were now providing a spiritual home were in danger of basing their lives on visions, specific words and feelings. We had to teach them the importance of the Scriptures so that they knew their lives were based firmly on truth. In this way they could learn to test the experiences they received and so avoid being deceived by the enemy.

Bob and I developed a 'Teaching for Life' Bible study course. In it we aimed to get across to all our members the great truths of what God had done in their lives. We also aimed to teach the practical, down-to-earth precepts of Scripture which are so relevant to our everyday living.

Most Christians were eager to learn. We all enjoyed it.

11

A wonderful mix

When Terry Virgo visited us in 1986 he commented on the wonderful mixture of people in the church. We thought so, too. Many widely differing cultures and jobs were represented.

We had people from the West Indies, Turkey, Holland, Mauritius, Nigeria, Ghana, New Zealand, Burma and India, not forgetting England, Ireland, Scotland and Wales. We had labourers, doctors, teachers, nurses, firemen, shop workers, window cleaners, accountants, factory workers, home helps, children, young families, single parents, older people and the middle-aged.

This variety led to some very interesting ideas. One New Year social stands out particularly – the whole church came in some form of national dress, two different countries being represented by each homegroup. In addition, appropriate ethnic food had been prepared.

Each group had members with direct links with at least one of those countries. A great time was had by all, not least in the sampling of the many foods.

Some of the weddings proved fascinating as different backgrounds and cultures met in marriage. We got used to expecting national customs to emerge and learned to understand and respect parents who weren't at all sure they agreed with our Christian weddings.

Integration of deaf Christians

God was about to add further to us. Visitors to our meetings are soon aware of a group of deaf people. An interpreter, using sign language, stands or sits at the front and relays everything to them. Their expressive faces as they hang on to every word are always a joy to everyone.

Like the rest of us, the deaf enjoy a good joke and will always laugh a few seconds after us, so we enjoy it twice! A number of hearing members have learnt sign language so that they can communicate. We sometimes laugh at them as they are visibly thrown by a long word or a difficult concept when interpreting the preaching.

Deaf Christians are always hungry for fellowship. The very nature of their disability cuts them off from others. They often have to travel miles before they find Christians with whom they can communicate.

In the old days, when we had united meetings, we noticed that they were always the last to leave. Now we are pleased to have the deaf Christians in our membership. It was in 1987 that they were welcomed in, but much had happened leading up to that time. We talked to Bert and Marie Barritt about it.

Bert was born in Bermondsey and had deaf parents. In 1957 God called him and his wife, Marie, into evangelistic work in Northern Ireland. So, together with their three children, they left their home in Catford and went, not knowing exactly to what. Within three months they found themselves part of a small but lively deaf fellowship in Belfast.

After spending three years there they received a clear brief from God to go back to London and duplicate what they had seen. Again they obeyed and over the next twenty years had the joy of seeing many deaf people saved and Deaf Christian Fellowship groups started all over the country. The story is exciting.

The first London group of the Deaf Christian Fellowship (DCF) met in Allerford Chapel in Catford for a time, sometimes joining with the hearing church there for baptisms. Then, after meeting in Victoria for several years and later in Bermondsey Gospel Mission, they finally settled into a building in Paradise Street, Rotherhithe, in the early 1970s.

Some deaf people came all the way from Ilford to Rotherhithe and so, after a few years, a separate congregation was planted in Ilford, with their own deaf pastor. The Rotherhithe fellowship also continued with a deaf pastor. Bert says that they worked all the time to make viable churches out of the groups of deaf Christians.

Throughout the time the DCF met in Bermondsey they joined in with united church meetings, getting together with BCF every three months. It was in 1985, Bert says, that God began to speak clearly about integrating the deaf into hearing churches.

'Give me back my church,' the Lord was saying. 'It's not good for the deaf to be alone.'

They were exhorted in prophecy to 'follow the cloud of God's glory' towards the hearing church. It took the leaders a little time to come to terms with the revelation. They had spent all those years geared to thinking of how to build up the deaf, and now God was saying, 'Hand them over.'

Questions were going through Bert's mind. How was it going to work? How would the deaf cope? How many would fall away? Were the hearing churches going to respond in the right way? Would they know what to do?

Bert says that, in spite of all his fears, he had always believed that the church should move on through prophetic input. He knew God was wanting a change of direction so they must move with him. That's how some deaf Christians came to Vineyard Community Church from Rotherhithe. Others moved to integrate into three or four other churches. Bert was thrilled that only two deaf members were 'lost in transit'.

'What we learned through all this,' he says, 'has revolutionised my thinking about the church. I want to develop the whole principle of integration. We are all under one Head, Jesus Christ. Acts 2:44 says that all the believers were together and had everything in common. This includes all the handicapped.

'Having all sorts of people together in the church is wholeness, and wholeness is part of God's restoration. God is reconciling the whole world to himself. There have been struggles and difficulties – they are part of the challenge – but deaf Christians are now entering into new dimensions of church life.'

The vision of our church is to see deaf and hearing people meeting regularly in the close fellowship of housegroups. For this to happen, we need more interpreters and others who can communicate with deaf people. Because of the present shortage of proficient interpreters, our deaf people meet together on some Sunday afternoons after our usual morning worship.

Integration is costly. Each one of us, deaf or hearing, needs to make the effort to understand one another.

Problems of growth

'Small is beautiful' was a phrase being bandied around at one time. We didn't like the huge comprehensive schools with well over a thousand pupils. Unless they were managed very well, pupils became just names on a register. The same applied to large local government bodies – they seemed remote from the needs of the people they were serving.

It had been nice to be in a small church where everyone knew each another and no-one was left out of anything. But now we were growing and it was a threatening situation for all of us.

In principle, most Christians are committed to growth. We want as many people as possible to find what we ourselves have found. We all sing with gusto such hymns as 'O for a thousand tongues to sing my great Redeemer's praise' and 'Flow, river, flow, flood the nations with grace and mercy'. I remember well the thrill of being part of a *Come Together* in the Albert Hall in the early 1970s. Worshipping with thousands of others gave us a taste of heaven. The same was true when we went to the Bible Weeks.

Yes, we longed for the church to grow, for many others to experience God for themselves. But we were not quite so sure when it began to dawn on us what that really meant for our small fellowship. We became aware of tensions within the church as we began to grow.

'There are so many people there on Sunday mornings,' people commented, 'that I just don't know who to try and get to know. Then, when I make an effort to do that, I don't get time to talk to the people I know well.'

'I'm afraid of welcoming a newcomer now because the last person I spoke to turned out to have been coming for over a month. I felt so embarrassed,' was a typical remark.

'Little things seem to go unnoticed,' said another. 'It's assumed that someone else is responsible, but nobody knows who.'

'I'm concerned that, as we grow bigger, individuals won't be cared for properly,' expressed still another.

'Some of these new people have such big problems that I'm afraid of being sucked under by them,' was a different fear.

The hard truth was beginning to hit us: there is a price to pay for growth. We were losing our cosy, safe little fellowship. Were we all willing to pay that price? It had been hard enough coping with just a few additions. Were we ready for a multiplication of numbers?

We encouraged our members to talk over these questions in homegroups. If we were committed to the vision for growth we must be prepared to reach out to new people who came on Sunday mornings. This demanded extra effort from us all; we couldn't be exclusive in our friendships. Each one of us needed to be prepared to talk to the person sitting next to us during a service. Shy people found this particularly hard.

Some problems could be dealt with by proper organisation. So, on the practical level, Bob and I appointed leaders for stewarding and administration teams.

In encouraging people to face their fears, we taught on the security in God which we enjoy as Christians. None of us would lose out if we committed ourselves fully to putting God's kingdom before our own comfort. We were all human, however, and needed to talk and pray about our particular fears, finding God's answers in the process.

Certainly, none of us wanted growth with a subsequent dilution of the love God had given us. It is written in Acts that the church was 'one in heart and mind'. If that could be true of a church with more than five thousand members, it could also be true of VCC! We needed constantly to remind our people, as the New Testament itself does, to 'love one another'. God would not have had this exhortation recorded as frequently unless he knew we would need it.

It was dangerously easy, now that we were a larger fellowship, to spend time only with people with whom we got on well. We encouraged members to watch out for the lonely and shy, seeking to increase their circle of friends.

Homegroups were smaller care units within the larger body. They were particularly important in seeing that no-one was left out as each member looked to the needs of others. The load of those with particular problems could be shared. In doing that, we tried to make it clear that they mustn't carry problems which ought to be passed on to leaders or elders. This discovery often released Christians into being more outgoing.

Leadership

Bob and I had been committed to bringing on younger leaders with whom we could share the responsibility. By 1987 we had a good, strong leadership team working together. These committed men and women were a great joy to us.

One of these younger leaders was David Nunn, who had been in leadership since the Lansdowne days. He had long known the call of God on his life and so, in April 1986, we acknowledged it by bringing him into eldership. Ray Lowe, from Biggin Hill, and John Houghton came and laid hands on him.

Meanwhile, tensions were arising in the leadership, mainly because there was no clear leader. Bob and I were very different in our approach to things and, while this had been an asset in the beginning, it was fast creating a bottle-neck. Because of our different leadership styles we were becoming a weight on each other and on the church.

The younger men were not sure how to relate to us at times. When a difference arose, it was easy to work out between the two of us, but it was far harder when more were involved. It gave particular problems to those nearest to us, often causing insecurity and misunderstandings. Also, with two experienced men at the top, budding preachers and teachers often felt there wasn't enough room for them.

Clearly something had to happen. I grappled in prayer before God. Sue and I prayed, 'Lord, do you want us here or is it time to go?'

We felt extreme weariness in our spirits. We were so immersed in the situation that it was difficult to see clearly. We needed the help of someone with apostolic gift. It came through Dave Holden from Sidcup, a member of Terry Virgo's apostolic team.

John Houghton had recently moved to Sussex, so Dave took his place in bringing oversight and counsel. After much talking and prayer, during which time the team also prayed, it was decided that I should be the one to look for another church. A number of other fellowships were in need of someone with a pastoral gift. The Lord confirmed in our spirits this course of action, and so I began to look elsewhere.

We remembered the sense of fulfilment we had experienced at the praise march the year before. By God's grace we had seen the fruit of his promise given in the 1960s. Even so, it was very hard to leave. Sue and I have found it easier to let go of our older teenagers than to let go of Vineyard. I think we will always have a little bit of our hearts in the inner city.

This has been our personal story, but the church of God is much bigger than individuals. Jesus is its Head and he has promised to build his house so that the gates of hell will not topple it. So the story of Vineyard goes on.

In 1988, almost twenty years after I went full-time at Lansdowne, I took up the leadership of a church in Shepperton, Middlesex. We received a very warm welcome and soon slotted into the fellowship, meeting their need for a full-time leader.

At my welcome meeting, along with other visitors, a large proportion of VCC turned out. It is good to know that all of us are part of God's worldwide family. It is an honour to serve him in it. We continue to look for his church to grow, wanting to prove his continuing faithfulness.

12

Just the beginning

'There was a blackbird singing on the roof of Pilgrim House,' Dr Oxford brightly began her annual medical report one year in the 1950s. She had been speaking to the supporters and subscribers of Lansdowne at the yearly meeting. Many who lived in the suburbs had been puzzled by her introduction. Why was it worth mentioning?

Dr Oxford went on to explain that, because of one single new law, London's air was cleaner. The blackbirds, after a long absence from inner London, were back, brightening the environment with their song.

The new law was the Clean Air Act of 1956. Smokeless zones had been created in which it was an offence to burn anything other than smokeless fuel. It effectively cut down the abundance of smoke from house and factory chimneys which had daily polluted the atmosphere.

No longer did Londoners have to suffer the 'pea-soupers', those dense smogs which caused such traffic chaos and death in the early 1950s. The blackbird's song heralded a new era for the birds. Slowly, other species returned to join the pigeons, starlings and sparrows. In fact, we were amazed one morning to see a heron perched on the roof of a nearby hospital, less than fifty yards from the busy main road.

Other changes have taken place. Even the London part of the River Thames now contains fish. Many famous buildings have been cleared of their grime, now displaying their former beauty. In some places, more trees have been planted and areas of grass surround the blocks of flats. The 'concrete jungle' has in some ways improved.

Fundamental change – how?

No-one would pretend, however, that the basic quality of life has improved. What new law will help reduce the level of violence, the crime and divorce rates? What will alleviate people's fear, loneliness and general unhappiness? What will curb the vandalism and graffiti, the drug-taking and the mutual disrespect?

Governments, town halls, educationalists and sociologists continue to put up various plans which may help. But only the gospel of Jesus Christ meets the needs of the whole person. Only Christ can change people from the inside, writing his law on their hearts, giving them righteousness, peace and joy in God's Holy Spirit.

New Testament churches

Christian evangelistic missions come and go. Christian philanthropic help meets a need here and there. But God's chosen way is through his church.

This book has been written out of a strong conviction that New Testament churches are the great need of the inner cities. A body of worshipping Christians moving under God's direction affects the lives of others, bringing dynamic change to whole communities.

I am even more convinced now than I was twenty years ago of the truth and relevance of the direction God has given. God took my willingness to serve him, developed my understanding and gradually and patiently opened my eyes to see more of his revealed purpose in his Word. I had to be willing to let him change me, deepening my experience of him and his church.

In Bermondsey I began to see what God had promised: 'Instead of the thornbush will grow the pine tree, and instead of briers the myrtle will grow.'

Recently an old friend introduced me to someone and spoke of my 'having done a great work in Bermondsey'.

I can't see that it has been me. Individuals don't usually achieve much on their own. What has been done is because I've been part of a body.

What of VCC's future? No church, no matter how full of God's grace in the past, can stand still, resting on what has gone before. Isaiah warns of the danger of not submitting to God's pruning and care. The result is small, sour grapes which are not pleasing to God (Isaiah 5). He plants his vineyards in order that they may produce good fruit.

For VCC the battle is still on. She will go from strength to strength as she obeys God and resists the enemy.

I believe the challenge is fourfold. First, to demonstrate a high quality of loving community life, centred on God's Spirit and his Word. Second, to continue reaching out to every group within local society. Third, to train leaders from those various groups. And, finally, to grow, and so make an increasing impact on society as a whole.

A drop in a bucket

At the time of writing, VCC has a hundred and fifty committed members, plus hoards of children! Locally it may be the largest protestant congregation but it is still only a drop in a bucket. In a small town, its size could have quite an impact; not so in a vast city. Most local people, even those living quite close, probably haven't even heard of it – it needs to grow.

Its growth must be not only in quantity but also in quality – maintaining the vision of love, unity and commitment to the Lord and to each other, remaining faithful to the Scriptures and moving freely with God's Spirit. Each individual Christian can then come to maturity in Christ, filled with his love.

I believe the church must continually look for ways of reaching out to meet social needs. Years ago God directed us to curtail our many activities so that we could get our own house in order. God has now equipped many of his local churches, far from perfect though they may still be, to stretch out towards needy people. We must look for church-based and Holy-Spirit-directed means of doing so.

That way, when new people come into the church they can truly find themselves – by learning to give and receive as part of a God-centred community.

Bermondsey is only one district in one of our great cities. There are many more needing strong New Testament churches.

'I still long to see a church planted in Walworth,' expressed one of our Christian brothers, his heart full of compassion for those around him.

I pray for a sustained, thoughtful, aggressive strategy of church-planting by men of apostolic gift, a strategy to which many more Christians will lend their efforts, whatever the cost.

'Are you willing to go and live in a terraced house if God wants it?' asked one Downs Bible Week speaker a few years ago.

'Yes, please!' joked some of our flat-dwellers.

Are *you* willing to go where God wants? To put up with rotten circumstances or to forgo some material 'traditions of men' for his kingdom's sake?

Part of a whole

In my early Christian days I saw each local church as an entity in itself, strongly independent and self-governing. I now see that each fellowship is also a part of a larger whole. We have been glad of the input from others.

I believe each local fellowship should support its own full-time leaders but I would also like to see churches in more affluent areas helping to support specific projects within poorer districts. For example, VCC now has three large buildings to maintain. Bracknell Baptist Church have tithed some of their own building fund to the church, thus helping to renovate the Drummond Road Baptist Church premises.

Sometimes, Christians from the leafy suburbs have made patronising comments or viewed the inner-city Christian as a super-hero. Neither attitude is helpful. But warm, genuine, prayerful interest and understanding is invaluable.

Finally

Sue and I can honestly say that we enjoyed our time in Bermondsey. We proved God's faithfulness in supplying all our needs, financial and otherwise. Sometimes it was painful, sometimes tiring, sometimes stressful, often exciting – but never boring.

Bermondsey is a place of great opportunity. Working for God there has been a privilege. He has spoken and established his church, using far-from-perfect Christians. Ultimately she will be presented to Jesus as part of his perfect, spotless bride.

Until then, we ask that he will continue to use her to turn many more from darkness to light.

GOOD BOOKS FROM HARVESTIME

Learning the Joy of Prayer
– How to spend one hour with God

by Larry Lea

Larry Lea's book continues to be a best-seller in the USA under its original title, *Could You Not Tarry One Hour?*

At a crucial stage in his life when he felt discouraged, depressed and lacking direction, God drew him to that most familiar of prayers, the Lord's Prayer. In obedience he repeated the familiar words. It took just twenty seconds. God urged him to do it again, but slowly.

Here commenced a voyage of discovery in which each phrase of the Lord's Prayer became an element in an outline for a time with God. Using the outline revolutionised his prayer-life. He was beginning to learn the *joy* of prayer.

Larry Lea's enthusiasm is infectious. Here you, too, can learn how to spend more time in prayer each day — and find joy in doing so.

ISBN 0 947714 76 6

£2.95